Mediumship

The Ultimate Guide to Becoming a Spiritual Medium and Developing Psychic Abilities Such as Clairvoyance, Clairsentience, and Clairaudience

Your Free Gift (only available for a limited time)

Thanks for getting this book! If you want to learn more about various spirituality topics, then join Mari Silva's community and get a free guided meditation MP3 for awakening your third eye. This guided meditation mp3 is designed to open and strengthen ones third eye so you can experience a higher state of consciousness. Simply visit the link below the image to get started.

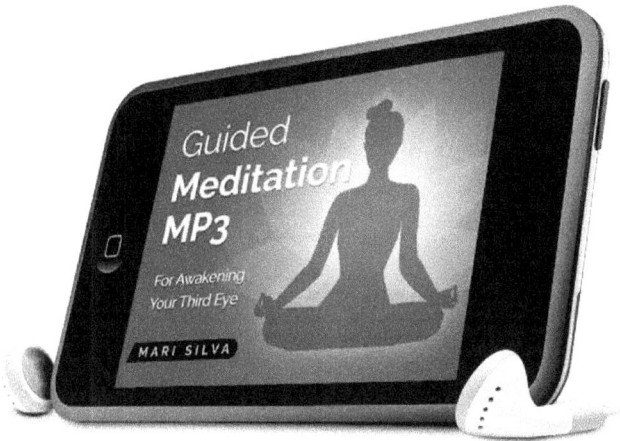

https://spiritualityspot.com/meditation

Contents

Introduction

"Who is a Medium?"

If someone asked you that, what would come to mind? Think beyond movies, plays, and fictional stories; how would you describe a medium? You probably have an inaccurate impression of mediums and mediumship, thanks to the media's misrepresentation. The typical depiction of mediums is that of a lone soul living in an isolated stone manor, surrounded by ghosts and spirits. In the movies, they look pale and frightening with an almost unearthly appearance.

A medium is just a regular person like you and me. Contrary to what many people believe due to conditioning, mediums are respectable people from different walks of life. The reality contrasts with what we all learned growing up. Unfortunately, the practice and its practitioners have been subjected to excessive dramatization for entertainment.

Mediumship is the ability to mediate between the spirit and human worlds. Mediums act as intermediaries between humans and spiritual beings on the "other side." The difference between you and a practicing medium is that they have trained themselves to be psychically attuned to the physical and spiritual planes.

Every human is born with the inherent gift to see beyond this material world into other dimensions. We tend to lose our connection with this natural gift as we grow older. The less we use the ability, the more we forget the basics. By the time we are adults, we have entirely cast the powers aside. Mediums can still access this ability, and that separates them from everyone else.

A medium is an earnest individual with spiritual knowledge, belief, desire, and patience, keen to make a difference in this world by connecting with ethereal beings in the metaphysical world.

Many people are skeptical of the paranormal because humans find it hard to understand things not supported by science. Yet, several established stories and reports about people who have genuinely had contacts with spirits and the spirit realm exist. Ask those people, and you will realize that science does not have all the answers.

This book aims to redefine your perception of mediumship and help facilitate an awakening of your inner psychical gifts. The ability to communicate with spirits is not farfetched if one stays within the realms of reality and possibility. This book sets a realistic expectation of what the journey is like for new mediums. Intended as a practical guide, it takes a sound approach in unraveling the fundamentals of mediumship. This pragmatic and down-to-earth guide is the right resource to launch your self-discovery journey.

This guidebook is for people who want practical tips that can be applied to their day-to-day lives to trigger remarkable personal and spiritual development. This is for those who need a resource that will change their lives. If you want a book that will teach you how to gain superpowers, this is not for you.

But do you want a practical handbook that can help you cultivate and hone the natural gift of mediumship that is embedded within your DNA? In that case, this is the book for you. Before you get started, make sure that you are ready to acknowledge there are more dimensions and realms beyond the one you see with your physical eyes. When you accept this, you will begin your attunement to your inner psychic!

Chapter One: Are You a Medium?

"We are all connected to spirit, in our physical manifestation and our soul."

—Linda Masanimptewa

Are you a medium? How do you know if you can contact spirits and ghosts? Are there signs you can observe? These are the most critical questions you must answer before you begin your mediumship.

Individuals new to this practice often want to know how they can strengthen their gifts. What they fail to realize is that this is not the starting point. You have to start by making sure that you indeed have the facilities to be a medium. Before I dive deep into how you can discover this, I want to clarify what mediums do.

Like the introduction made clear, mediums can psychically communicate with deceased people on the other side. The general belief is that mediums speak to the dead, but this is a misconception. There is no "death." The dead do not exist. If death were real, everyone would disappear into oblivion after their souls pass on to another realm. What we know as death is the transition of humans from physical entities to a spiritual state.

Mediums are the people who are intuitive and sensitive enough to access information from the dimension where spirits transit to using their psychic senses. These allow them to see, feel, and hear any communication attempt from spirit realms.

Now, it's time to go back to establishing whether you can connect with spirits or not. I have pointed out that we are all born with inherent psychic ability. But you can be psychic without being a medium. One of the most common misconceptions is that psychics and mediums are the same. There is an essential distinction between them. Understanding this is the foundation to becoming an authentic medium.

A medium may be psychic, but a psychic isn't necessarily a medium. This distinction is one that people tend to ignore, willfully or otherwise. I started this chapter by highlighting this difference because it is the right place to begin. I have met many people who confuse the two, and this often affects their psychic development journey.

Many people think that mediumship should come to them naturally because they have the gift of intuition. The fact remains that unless you are a natural-born medium, you have to put a lot of work into developing this ability.

The difference between a medium and a psychic is that mediums can raise their vibrational frequency to where they connect with the spirit world. But psychics can access information about the past, present, and future, but not by connecting with the other side; a psychic uses their ability to communicate with the higher planes.

Some people are psychic with the gift of mediumship and are called psychic mediums. A psychic medium has a double ability to speak to the deceased and learn information from the higher planes.

Furthermore, there are natural-born mediums and latent mediums. A natural-born medium has always been in tune with their abilities. Even though they may not realize it, natural-born mediums tend to see signs that point to this gift throughout their childhood into adulthood.

In contrast, a latent medium is someone whose ability stays dormant until it is developed later in life. Most people I have met tend to be latent mediums. Typically, latent mediums get signs and can use their ability from childhood. But as they grow older, the gifts become dormant and lost to them.

Anyone who is psychic has a propensity for spirit channeling. If you have psychic senses, then you can speak to ghosts. Being psychically attuned from birth makes no difference in this context. What matters is your willingness to learn and your eagerness to try.

How to Tell if You Are a Medium

Communicating with those who have passed away is the hallmark of mediumship. One way you can tell is if you have already seen ghosts, apparitions, or spirits in your life.

The first step is to look back into your childhood. Growing up, you must have had specific fears. Examine them. You may find that your childhood fears are tied to your inclination toward psychic ability. You might be a medium if:

- You had a fear of the dark as a child. Usually, predisposed children have a persistent fear of the dark, resulting from their subconscious awareness of the paranormal.

- You dreaded sleeping in a room alone due to vivid nightmares.

Then consider your play patterns as a child. What did you like to do? When you don't remember, ask your parents. Without realizing it, you might have had individual experiences that tilt toward the supernatural. Ask your parents if you had an imaginary friend while growing up. Supposing the answer is yes, it could mean you always interacted with a friendly spirit (or spirits) then. Often, adults see their kids seemingly interacting alone and conclude that they have "imaginary friends."

Examine Your Interests - If you had a strong interest in understanding meaning and religion, this could be another sign of your psychic connection. As a child, you might have:

- Asked parents or guardians to explain different religious beliefs to you.

- Engaged in activities that involved playing with psychic tools like tarot cards or a Ouija board.

- Read spiritual-themed or supernatural-themed books.

The older you grow, the more profound the signs become. Reflect on your middle age. Mediums tend to see auras and symbols around living people and objects. An aura is an invisible energy field surrounding everything in the universe. Most people cannot see the aura, but those in touch with their psychic side can. Seeing an aura is a sign of clairvoyance, one of the significant psychic senses that mediums have. So, think about the thing (s) that you see around others.

Understand the feeling you get when you are around other people. Can you sense people's presence in a room even before seeing them? If you can do this, it is a sign you are clairsentient. Like clairvoyance, clairsentience is also a dominating psychic sense in mediums. It is the ability to feel or sense people's energy and moods. As a clairsentient:

- You are deeply intuitive about people's feelings, thoughts, and moods.

- Touching or holding an item owned by another person makes you feel an overwhelming connection to their emotions and experiences.

Most mediums typically have personal experiences relating to death. Having a near-death encounter is how people discover their gifts. If this has never happened to you, remember the loved ones you have lost. If you have medium powers, losing a loved one can trigger strange occurrences.

An example of this could be odd sensations and feelings or something as dismissible as suddenly slammed doors. Suppose you have experienced something similar before. In that case, that might have been the spirit of your deceased loved one trying to communicate with you.

Realizing the gift you have is no easy feat. It is a long and complicated process. So many people are still unaware of their abilities. For some people, their gifts might not become clear to them until they are at a certain age. Most have experiences they believe are familiar to everyone else.

Suppose you persistently sense and feel things that rarely mean anything to you. There, they could make a difference in the lives of people around you. The messages you receive from spirits may or may not have anything to do with you in particular. Sometimes, souls choose specific people to relay messages to because they are accessible to them.

You may not relate to any of the signs mentioned above; that takes nothing away from your potential to be gifted. It does not mean you don't have the ability – it only suggests that you need to tap into your subconscious and awaken that part of you.

Everyone can connect with their loved ones who have passed away. Spirit is always willing to interact with anybody. You have to make yourself more open to the connection. To do this, you have to strengthen your awareness and pay more attention to the things around you.

Certain things could happen to you like a coincidence or a strange occurrence, but you may find they remind you of someone you have lost if you pay attention. These are often signs and symbols. Unless you immerse yourself in your environment, you will miss out on these cues from spirit.

Not all mediums know their abilities. Some require a little nudge to awaken their potential. If you fall under that category, there are things you can do to find your psychic muscle. Knowingly or unknowingly, you might even have been doing things to tap into your intuitive senses.

The number one thing that obstructs an individual from learning of their gifts is fear. Fear hinders you from opening yourself to your innate skills. Once they see supernatural signs, many get so scared that they subconsciously shut it out. But it is vital to understand these experiences are not scary. You shouldn't fear what you don't comprehend. Instead, actively try to make sense of it.

Psychic skills shouldn't cause you to fear. They are there to assist you on the path to awakening and higher consciousness. Thus, the first step to tapping into your potentials is opening yourself up to the possibilities. Embrace your otherworldly capabilities. Let the universe know that you are ready to explore your gifts. Do not allow fear to dictate your reaction to the knowledge of the ethereal.

The second thing you can do is to be more attuned to energy. When you meet someone new, there is a "vibe" you get. The "vibe" in this context is the energy. Everyone has the intuitive ability to sense someone's energy. That is how you can tell whether the stranger you meet is trustworthy or not.

Sensing a person's vibe is a manifestation of your inner psychic intuition. It indicates that you indeed have the ability, and you need to exercise it more. Strengthening that skill is all you need. So, challenge yourself to read and interpret people's energy purposively. Look beyond the appearance and disposition to find the true person.

Tapping into a person's energy will give you more information about them than you will find anywhere else.

How, you might wonder? Be in their presence and be mindful of the way you feel. Understand how this reflects on them. You don't even have to see or interact with the person to do this. For example, if you are in a queue to enter a cinema, deliberately tap into anybody's energy around you and see what you find. Then start a conversation to substantiate the findings of your little energy probe.

Clairvoyance is one of the dominant psychic abilities in mediums. Practicing psychic seeing is another method for tapping into your inner potentials. One of the best ways to practice is to use a remote-viewing exercise. You practice "seeing" things from a distance. Whenever you have to visit a new place, try remote viewing ahead of your visit. Close your eyes and visualize the location in your head. Try to "see" this location, then put down whatever appears in your mind's eye.

Later, when you get to the actual place, compare your imagined description of the area to its real look. Don't be surprised when you discover that you got some of the shapes or features right. Your visualization may be precise, with certain things in the exact spots you imagined them.

To further tune into your gifts, facilitate contact with spirit guides. Spirit guides are higher-dimensional beings that are assigned uniquely to you. They exist to support and guide you in every endeavor, and many have survived multiple lifetimes on this plane. You have different spirit guides, ranging from angels to spirit animals. Each guide offers a distinctive blend of knowledge, wisdom, and skills.

Usually, one gets up to six guides that serve different purposes. One spirit guide may be for protection, another for healing, and another to help you achieve an objective. They also exist to aid you in developing your psychic gifts. That is the guide to call upon when striving to unlock your latent medium. In a later chapter, I will elucidate more on how you can contact your spirit guides.

Now, you may be wondering exactly why one could want to establish a connection with the spirit world. What do you stand to benefit from contacting otherworldly beings? The answer to this question is at the very heart of mediumship.

Being a medium allows you to lessen the pain and grief of the bereaved. With your ability, you can offer them comfort. Merely knowing that the spirits of their deceased loved ones are around to watch over them can assuage the guilt felt by grieving families.

Mediumship allows you to pray for or help to transition a departed soul. Sometimes, souls become anchored to the Earth and cannot transit to the other side. That often happens due to something else acting as a tether to keep them bound here. By communicating with a medium, these spirits can solve the anchoring issue and move on to eternal peace.

Acting as an intermediary between this world and the spirit world is a way you can gain and improve esoteric knowledge. To undergo full spiritual awakening and enlightenment, talking to spirits who have been in other dimensions might be the place to start. Channeling energies is also a way for you to establish a dialogue with the metaphysical world. You can create a bridge between this world and the spiritual ones.

In some instances, the departed comes seeking to communicate with the living. They do this for several reasons, which include:

- Assuring their loved ones they are okay. This mostly happens when the departed lose their souls through an accident or other equally traumatic events.
- To provide help and assistance to the living.
- Curiosity and interest.
- See an unfinished business to the end

There are several other reasons spirits initiate contact with the living. These are just a few of the most common ones.

Do not be discouraged if you haven't experienced or witnessed anything that might be remotely related to psychic ability. You have probably had one or two experiences unknowingly. Using the tips given above, you can tap into your inherent psychic senses to trigger a fresh experience.

The most important thing is to make sure that mediumship is something you want for yourself. Look within yourself for the answer because that is the only place you will find it. If you proceed, be ready to believe and open yourself to all possibilities. Belief is essential. Without a robust belief system, your heart and mind will remain closed to spirit, making channeling impossible.

Last, understand that becoming a spiritual medium is a long process that requires you to study, practice, and, more importantly, be consistent. Learning a new skill requires consistency. Think of mediumship as a new skill you are just starting to learn. I guarantee you can completely redefine your perception and idea of this life when you reach a specific knowledge level in this field.

The next chapter dives deep into the different types of mediums and what makes each unique. How do you know which one you are? Let's find out!

Chapter Two: Types of Mediums

"Mediumship channels guidance from those who have gone before, not only for the sake of those who are here but also for those yet to come."

−Anthon St. Marteen

Mediumship is a far cry from what most people believe it to be. It manifests in people differently. Hence, there are various types of mediums. Although the end goal is to obtain information from the spiritual plane, all mediums are different. There are four types of medium. The kind of medium you become depends on your dominant psychic trait.

Humans intuit in four ways – through thoughts, feelings, energy, or the physical body. A person who intuits through emotions is an emotional intuitive. A mental intuitive absorbs thoughts and mental energy. A spiritual intuitive intuits via the human energy field, and a physical intuitive intuits by absorbing energy into the material body. Most people have all four means of intuition. Yet, there is a tendency to be more predisposed to one or two than the others.

As a medium, you connect and interact with the spiritual dimension through these intuitive channels. Your medium type depends on which of the four intuitive channels you use to communicate with the other side. In other words, your innate intuitive type determines the kind of medium you are. Knowing this is vital because it is the key to further developing your gifts.

Naturally, you are likely to have a predominant medium type. Still, you have probably experienced the distinctive connection phenomena of all four types. Below is a detailed insight into the different types of mediums based on the four intuitive modalities.

Emotional Medium

An emotional medium absorbs the emotional energy of spirits, often without realization. They can feel the range of emotions and feelings expressed on the other side better than any other medium type. Suppose you have ever had an influx of healthy, loving emotions with no idea of the source. There, you may be an emotional medium.

Have you ever been overwhelmed by a higher love that seems to come from another place? Do you continuously get vivid memories of a departed loved one that invoke a powerful emotional reaction in you? When spirits are around you, they invoke feelings of warmth and happiness that make you feel like someone else is in the room with you.

The above are ways that emotional mediums attune to the spirit world. Unknowingly, they connect with those who have passed on to the other side.

Emotional mediums are empathetic and compassionate, with a strong desire to make a difference in others' lives. They are in tune with the highest planes where divine love originates. They tend to be natural-born empaths, which makes clairsentience their predominant intuitive sense.

Being an empath makes them feel other people's emotions just as intensely as they feel their own, or that sometimes happens when they think those feelings are theirs. Not only can they tune into the emotional energy and feelings of physical dimensional beings, but they can also tune into the auras of those in the higher spiritual realms to access emotional information.

The primary way emotional mediums receive messages from the spirit world is through feelings and emotional sensations. Suppose you are an emotional medium. In that case, you may receive a sudden sense of warmth within you. Or you may feel unexplainably happy. When this happens frequently, it may mean that a cheerful spirit is trying to pass a positive message to you or another person you know.

To determine whether you are an emotional medium, try the exercise below.

- Comfortably sit on a chair or the ground. Close your eyes, then take a couple of long breaths. Deeply breathe in and out until you feel relaxed.

- Think of a loved one that is no more. Say the loved one's name out loud for the universe to hear. You may also say it silently. It is your choice to make.

- Continue breathing to keep yourself relaxed and calm. Feel the warmth of your breath as it goes in and out of your stomach.

- Open your heart and call your loved one's name again. Quietly, listen through your heart and wait.

- Allow your heart to receive the love and warmth your loved one's soul sends

- Listen for any other message they may be sending

- Send them a warm feeling of love from your heart

Practice this every day to sharpen your connection with the departed and the spiritual dimension. Whenever you get an unanticipated feeling, take time to observe the feeling. Try to decipher the message you are receiving. If you include this exercise in your daily schedule, it will strengthen your emotional link to the other side. Inadvertently, this will make spiritual messages more accessible to you.

Mental Medium

Although most people still can't distinguish between mediums, mental mediums are more known than any other medium type. As a mental medium, you unknowingly converse with spirits within your mind. Sometimes, the "conversation" is in the form of a vision playing out on a movie screen.

Psychic messages via the thoughts come at any time. It may occur while you are driving to work or running to the park. It does not matter what you are doing at that moment. Since communication happens through your thoughts, nothing can restrict or limit the connection.

Receiving others' thoughts is second nature to a mental intuitive. Due to this, you may not even realize when you communicate with spirits on the other side. Once you recognize and acknowledge that the conversations happening in your mind are more than just internal monologue, your ability develops more rapidly.

From that point, you can discern your thoughts from those of another being or entity. You might hear a voice that sounds like your own inside your mind, but that is probably a spirit trying to communicate. The voice may seem to you like that of a departed family member or loved one. Think back to the time when you heard someone call your name, but you could find no one in your vicinity. That is an instance of a departed projecting their voice into your mental auric layer.

Mental mediums have the gift of claircognizance, which translates to "clear knowing." The psychic sense allows you to know information and knowledge without a clue about the origin. Having claircognizance as your predominant psychic modality means you can communicate with ethereal beings through your thoughts. You may know the thoughts, ideas, and beliefs of a loved one on certain subjects without a clear idea of how you have this information.

Try the exercise below to determine if you are a mental medium.

- Close your eyes. Take a few deep breaths, then open your eyes.

- Think of an aspect of your life where you want a spiritual dimensional being's opinions.

- Write down a question or concern you want your departed friend to address.

- Then, write down the solutions and possibilities you have in mind. The point of this is to clear your mind and be open to the thought energy you are about to receive from the other side.

- Now, close your eyes again. Take a few deep breaths to keep your mind relaxed.

- Call out the name of the loved one with whom you seek a connection. Repeat the name three times.

- Ask your questions and repeat them three times. Repeating the question thrice ensures the spirits hear you correctly.

- Focus on your thoughts as you continue to relax. Listen for any message.

Write down every thought that emerges and be aware of any voice in your head. The thoughts that surface is quite possibly from the spirit with whom you are communicating.

Note they may differ from what you imagined or expected.

Spiritual Medium

A spiritual medium is capable of "seeing" spirits and departed souls. They tend to communicate with the spirit realm through dreams and daydreams. They can do this because their dominant psychic sense is clairvoyance, which means "clear seeing." Clairvoyance allows spiritual mediums to receive visual messages from the other side. Spiritual mediums typically receive intuitive drops in ways I would describe as elusive.

Being a spiritual medium means that your connection with the spirit planes may feel dreamy, almost to where you feel like it is imagined. With clairvoyance as your main psychic channel, you may have seen ghosts, spirits, and other ethereal beings and dismissed it as your eyes playing tricks.

Spiritual mediums have a depth of wisdom, which allows them to learn life lessons and purpose intuitively. As a spiritual medium, you can intuit your life's purpose and that of those around you. You need not visit psychics to discover specific things about yourself.

Having the gift of inner sight enables you to see energy, figuratively, symbolically, or realistically. You can see departed loved ones in their spirit form. This ability either happens through your inner sight or in the form of translucent beings. Sometimes, they can appear to you as three-dimensional figures in this realm.

Here is an exercise specifically for developing your gift of clear seeing and spiritual mediumship.

- Sit in a comfortable position.

- Close your eyes and breathe in deeply. Then breathe out just as deeply. Repeat the breathing exercise a couple of times to calm and clear your mind.

- Visualize a white orb of energy surrounding you. Imagine yourself hidden in the white light.

- As you keep taking deep breaths, envision the orb expanding and filling up with vibrant energy.

- Envision a loved one from the spirit realm coming into the orb. Call out the name of the person you want in the white light with you. Repeat the name a couple of times.

- Continue to take relaxing breaths as you repeat the spirit's name.

- At that moment, you may feel warm tingling-like energy passing through your nerves. Or you may see a symbol or image of the person. Sometimes, the spirit may appear as a streak of sparkling light.

- You may try to initiate a conversation with the spirit or simply open your mind to the message he or she has for you.

Spiritual mediumship is the same as healing mediumship. You can raise your vibrational levels to the height of consciousness, where you can channel divine energy from the spiritual realms. Furthermore, you can impart the energy in a living person to initiate healing. The standard way to do this is to channel the divine energy through your body to another person's body.

Many people believe that spirit mediums are the most potent types of mediums, but no medium type is more powerful than the others. The extent of your abilities depends strictly on how you train yourself. It has nothing to do with how you connect with the spiritual dimension.

Physical Medium

The defining trait in physical mediums is their ability to interact with spirits through their gut feelings. Spiritual messages come to them in the form of physical sensations. An excellent example of this is when the hairs on your arms stand up while reminiscing about a deceased loved one. Perhaps you have had gut feelings that a departed friend or family member is present. You may sense they are standing behind you or simply get a sensation of their warm hand on your back. These are just some ways that spirits connect with physical mediums.

Assume you are a physical medium. In that case, you can tangibly interact with spirits and otherworldly entities. Souls that have passed have a knack for things such as blinking lights, dropping items on our path, and ringing the doorbell for no reason. Although these happen to many mediums, they usually occur more often to physical mediums.

Physical mediums are adept at psychometry, which is the ability to intuit energy from an object. When you look at a deceased person's photo, you can get a lot of information about them if you are a physical medium. How is this possible? Physical mediumship makes you more connected to the impermeable physical vibrations from the spirit world. The connection gives physical mediums a psychic advantage over all other types of mediums.

Information intuited through physical vibrations comes as a gut feeling or knowing, a sense of a spirit's presence, or through the gift of inner sight. Any message sent from the other side triggers specific physical sensations in your body, causing you to pay attention.

Below is an exercise for physical mediums. Try this to check the extent of your physical attunement to the unseen dimension.

- Find an object belonging to a deceased family member or friend. This object should naturally be something they cherished dearly while on Earth. It could be a ring or necklace. You may also use a photo of the deceased for this exercise.

- Close your eyes and do a quick breathing exercise.

- As usual, call out or silently mutter the name of the spirit you wish to contact.

- Gently open your eyes and stare purposefully at the photo or personal item.

- Sharpen your awareness and pay attention to sensations in your body.

- You may feel or sense their presence or feel a rush of energy breeze by you. You may glimpse a silhouette of your loved one as a streak of sparkling light or color. You may also hear their voice.

Even if you receive no signs of a psychic message on your first try, don't stop the exercise. Keep trying until your first breakthrough. Remember that the ability is somewhere within you. Therefore, it is not about having it – but about *tapping into it.*

Knowingly or unknowingly, you may have experienced these types of interactions with entities in the unseen world. So, how exactly do you know which medium type you are?

In my experience, the best way to decipher your medium type is to observe which experience you have more than others. If you always seem to know things that were never in your head, you could be a mental medium. If not, you may be the other medium types.

Essentially, the one thing that matters is that you can intuit through your thoughts, feelings, energy, and physical body. Therefore, you can be any medium you want. Remember that it is okay to be predisposed to one medium type than the others. It takes nothing away from your abilities. It adds a lot to you.

As you become more self-conscious of your natural connection, you will become more confident in your medium abilities. This makes them effortless to hone. One vital thing you shouldn't forget is that you must never compare yourself to other mediums. Doing that to yourself is a way of undermining your potentials.

Mediumship is like a skill, as I mentioned before. Everyone learns a new skill at an individual pace. So, in your journey to spiritual self-discovery, don't distract yourself by comparing your success with that of another medium. Focus on your gifts and the difference you can make with them in your life and other people's lives.

Chapter Three: Beginning Your Psychic Journey

"We only receive in a psychic reading what is most necessary and beneficial to us at that particular moment in time. Nothing more. Nothing less."

−Anthon St. Marteen

Intuitive guidance and psychic abilities come naturally. Still, psychic development is a journey with a specific destination in mind. This means there are several roads you must take on your way. There are steps you must take on the path to psychic development. Remembering that mediumship is a type of psychic ability, this chapter is written from a general psychic perspective.

Having a psychic predisposition is a state of being. It is less about doing and more about being. But most people make psychic development more complicated than it is. It happens because they have had no proper guidance as beginners. Knowledge about the psychic voyage can make your path more straightforward and far less complicated than for those who do not have this knowledge.

Know there are varying ways you can incorporate intuitive development into your daily activities. It is the best way to master your abilities because everyday use strengthens your trust in these activities. It would help if you did a few things before beginning your development journey are basic things you may otherwise ignore. I have six things I always suggest people do before they get started.

It may come as a surprise, but the first thing is to declutter. That's right - you need to clear your physical and mental spaces. Relieving your living/working space and your mind of stuff that no longer benefits you is crucial to spiritual awakening. Clutter encourages distraction. Remembering that focus is essential to psychic development; you cannot have clutter anywhere around you. While decluttering your physical space, you must declutter your mind. The best way to rid the mind of unwanted thoughts and beliefs is to meditate every single day.

Meditation is food for the soul. It is the practice of sitting in silence and solitude to achieve mindfulness. During meditation, allow your thoughts to flow freely. Don't stifle, repress, or judge any of your thoughts. Let them pass without judgment. Slowly, your mind will become free of mental clutter.

Meditation is a way of grounding yourself to be present in the moment - which is present and valid - without worries about anything. When you immerse yourself in the present, you will realize there is no fear, only love. This realization offers you a more vital link to your intuitive self.

Examining your beliefs is also something you do before starting your psychic practice. Be intentional about the journey you are about to take. Know what you believe in. Acknowledge that you are affecting your world and the world at large with your energy. Make sure that your beliefs match the spiritual growth and awakening you are about to experience.

Often, intuitive development requires that one lets go of certain beliefs that have been there from inception. Fortunately, that is the thing about psychic awakening - first, realize that you have been asleep all along.

Again, expand your mind to the possibilities of the path you are on. Opening your mind is key to achieving an intuitive journey. A closed mind cannot be visited or affected by spirit. The point of a psychic awakening is to help you learn something new. It is unachievable if you don't open and expand your mind to your potential and the realms you experience.

Energy is everywhere around you, but you will find it outside more. So, prepare to spend more time outdoors. Spirit and energy are awaiting you in nature. Many people want to become psychics, yet they spend all their time sitting indoors behind a MacBook screen. How can you connect with the world if you never spend your time in it?

Connecting with nature is a surefire way to prepare for the journey. Understand that spirits love nature, so spending time in nature can help amplify your psychic portals to the spirit plane. When you connect with nature, put your mobile gadgets away to avoid distractions. Soak yourself in the quiet and solitude. You may surprise yourself.

This one often sounds odd to many but eating a healthy diet is vital to psychic development. One can write a whole book on the importance of healthy eating to psychic awakening and growth. The foods you eat can block your energy centers, resulting in an imbalance of your spiritual body. Blocked energy centers make the free flow of energy through the soul, body, and mind impossible. In turn, this leads to a limitation of your psychic abilities.

Healthy eating allows you to stay attuned to the Divine power and your inner guidance. So, add high-vibrational foods to your diet. Consume more vegetables and fresh fruit. They will keep your vibrational energy high, making it easier to connect to spirit. That does not mean you have to overhaul your whole diet; you only need to incorporate more high-vibe food. Examples include fruit, greens, and dark chocolate. You will notice a difference in how in-tune you are with your psychic abilities.

One cannot force a psychic awakening. With the right tips and guidance, anyone can go through one. But there is no definitive way to enlightenment. You cannot force your abilities to come alive, as you only do what you can do.

You may become too attached to the idea of becoming a psychic, medium, or psychic medium. In that case, your chances of experiencing it drop until it is nonexistent.

As a bonus, use your waiting time for more productive things. "Waiting time" is the period you spend waiting for the doctor in the waiting room or in the car waiting for your kids to finish school. That is a time you can use efficiently to develop your psychic senses, particularly clairaudience. Clairaudience is the psychic gift of "clear hearing." Doing this is better than just sitting around until the children get out of school or until it is your turn to see the doctor.

Once you know and understand all these things, it is time to begin your psychic journey. On your way to spiritual growth and advancement, three things must always be your companions. These include - meditation, visualization, and journaling. One by one, let's find out why they are crucial to your journey.

Meditation

I briefly highlighted the significance of meditation, but let's dive in deeper. There are many benefits of meditation for psychics. It is safe to say that these benefits are endless. There are vital advantages specifically for those on a psychic and spiritual development journey.

1. Connect to Your Higher Self

Your Higher Self knows who you are and why you are here on Earth. More important, it also knows the purpose of your psychic gifts. Meditation is the best way to connect with that all-knowing part of you. When you meditate, you open layers of yourself that you didn't know existed. It is a way of diving deep and focusing on your inner self. Since your Higher Self is the spiritual part of you, meditation automatically brings you there.

2. Remove Negative Energy

Psychics must always attract positive energy. Just like you clean your house, your energy field also requires daily cleaning. Meditation is the best way to rid yourself of harmful and toxic energy. It is a way to get rid of internal cobwebs and clouds of dust so you can refocus your mind on what is truly important. Not only does meditating kick negativity and toxicity to the curb, but it also raises your vibrations. This ushers in the sense of calm and grounding that is attractive to spiritual beings.

3. Achieve Emotional Balance

Emotional balance is crucial when one is on a spiritual journey. Again, it is a way to raise your vibration. Meditation helps take your focus from your past so you can focus on your present as it is. That fresh perspective triggers emotional balance, resulting in an alignment of your logical self and spiritual self. It is proof that psychic practices do not counter logic in any way. If anything, they promote the use of reason.

4. Heighten Your Intuition

Intuition is the channel through which the nonphysical part of you communicates with Spirit. Daily meditation can help enhance your intuition by bridging the gap between you and your Higher Self.

The question is, how do you meditate?

You have to meditate to get the benefits discussed above. So, how do you meditate the right way? There are no benefits to gain if you do your meditation incorrectly. If you have never meditated before, starting with a guided meditation can help make sure you get it right. It is a way to make things easy for yourself.

The best thing about it is that you don't have to think or worry about anything. It is all spelled out for you. Just follow the instructions. There are apps for guided meditations you can easily find online. Try the different apps until you find one suited to your liking.

Meditating is straightforward. Find a quiet and comfortable place where you can be in solitude. You can choose a specific area in your home for daily meditative practice. It is all about grounding yourself in the moment. One way to do this is to focus on your breathing and calmly allow your thoughts to pass through without distracting from your breath. Besides that, you can also focus on a specific mantra. The endgame is to fully immerse yourself in the present, up to where you are aware of everything happening around you.

During meditation, your mind may wander to other things. It is usual for this to happen. Redirect your mind back to the object of concentration whenever you find it wandering. The three tips for using guided meditation are:

- Sit in a comfortable spot with a good headphone plugged in your ears

- Focus entirely on the guided meditation

- Bring back your mind to the guide whenever it wanders

If you would rather meditate the traditional way, follow the steps below.

- Sit quietly on a chair or the ground. Choose a position comfortable for you.

- Allow your thoughts to leave your mind. Visualize them floating on little clouds away from your mind.

- Place your palms on your tummy.

- Take deep breaths in and out. Focus on the rise and fall of your belly each time you inhale and exhale.

- Do this until your mind is clear and free of clutter

If the above makes you susceptible to incessant mind wandering, consider counting from 100 to 1 as you inhale. You can also chant a mantra as you meditate.

Tools that can make meditation better include:

- Meditation beads (Malas)
- Salt lamp
- Essential oils such as Lavender, Rose, Frankincense, Patchouli, and an oil diffuser
- Meditation mat

Having the items above can make meditation a fun and enlightening experience for you.

Visualization

Most people argue that visualization is just another type of meditation, but it is much more than that. Yes, you can integrate it into your daily meditative routine, but it can stand on its own. It involves using imagery and visuals to achieve mindfulness. It has all the benefits of meditation but is more vital to developing your psychic sense of clairvoyance. Awakening your inner sight requires you to practice exercises targeted at your mind's eye.

There are different visualization exercises you can use to sharpen your inner sight. You don't have to learn all these techniques. Just committing one or two to memory can make all the difference you want. Below are two exercises to train your psychic eye.

Exercise 1: Basic Visualization

This exercise is all about internal visualization. But then, all visualization techniques are somewhat internally generated. From the name, one may assume this basic method is easy to learn. But that depends on your work ethic. With consistency, it's easy to master. If you don't strive to be consistent, learning it may be challenging.

Practice is the key to progress. So, even if it is just five minutes of your whole day, make sure you get this exercise done daily.

• Find a calm and friendly spot, close your eyes, and start breathing steadily. Focus on your breath as it goes in and comes out. Do this for at least 2 minutes.

• Picture a place in your head – this could be anywhere from your favorite hangout place to your school. Just picture a familiar place. Imagine yourself in that place and look around.

• Visualize the scene with more specific detail. Imagine people walking by, breeze blowing, or birds chirping in nearby trees. You may even attempt to communicate with someone with you.

• Once you successfully interact within that scene, imagine yourself walking away from the place into the room where you are currently doing your visualization exercise.

• Further, imagine yourself sitting down to the exact place you are now seated. It should feel like you have just merged your real self and your imagined self.

Don't use the same scene for your daily practice. Otherwise, your mind will become used to that scene. When this happens, it means that your mind no longer actively participates in the process due to familiarity. That defeats the purpose you are visualizing. So, try different scenes every day. As you become better at visualization, try to include more details in the process. It will further strengthen your inner eye.

Exercise 2: Third Eye Visualization

This exercise aims at opening your inner clairvoyant. This is also basic because it is primarily for new practitioners. For this technique, be sure to sit or lie down. If you tend to go off to sleep easily, sit instead of lying down.

- Relax your body by doing your essential breathing exercise.

- Once you feel relaxed physically and mentally, bring your focus to your breathing. Imagine your breath getting lighter with each inhale and exhale. Visualize all the tension leaving your body as you exhale.

- After a few seconds, move your attention to the spot between your eyebrows. That is the home of your third eye. Remember to keep your physical eyes closed. Use your mind's eye to focus on that spot.

- Visualize a ball of glowing purple light around your head. Imagine the purple light growing bigger and bigger.

- Picture your pineal gland as a glowing little space in the middle of your head.

- Imagine a sparkling white light flowing out of your pineal gland. You should start feeling a warm, tingling sensation in the area around the center of your head. It means that your third eye is awakening.

- Once you feel ready to complete your meditation, slowly twitch or wiggle your toes and fingers. Then, gently open your eyes and take a couple of relaxing breaths.

Note: If your third eye spot suddenly feels too uncomfortable or overheated, pause the exercise immediately. You may also put a wet cloth over that area and breathe in your favorite essential oil.

Journaling

Journaling is one thing that new intuits ignore because they don't understand its importance. Yet, it is an essential part of any psychic journey. An individual's psychic awakening is not complete without it. It helps you achieve clarity, enhance your intuition, and mentally declutter as you progress in your path. These are just some of the most common benefits.

Before you engage in actual mediumship activities such as channeling spirits or ghosts, purchase a journal and pens. It might sound like an unimportant step, but I assure you it is not something to take lightly.

Don't just buy any journal. Get one that speaks to you. Connecting with your journal makes you want to open it and write things down every day. Your journal is unique to you and is a means of sharing your experiences with the spirit world, which means it should reflect your taste and personality. I recommend getting a celestial journal.

I should note you need not get a physical journal. You can also write on your phone or computer. But writing in a spiritual journal is much more personal. And it gives less room for distractions. There should be nothing to pull your mind away when recording your psychic experiences with the spirit world.

An important thing to note is that journaling must come naturally. Do not force the process. It is okay to feel stuck when you just get started. If that happens to you, don't push yourself. Growing up, we learn to filter our words before we speak or write. Due to this, we find it difficult to express ourselves through unfiltered words. Well, when it comes to psychic journaling, getting rid of your filters is essential. No-filter is what you need.

You have to allow yourself to get into the flow. If you can't get into the flow, pause your writing until you can. Pour out your thoughts exactly as they surface. Do not censor or stop a particular thought because it doesn't fit your expectation. Being a beginner, consider buying a journal that comes with writing prompts. It will ensure you don't feel stuck every time you have to write.

Meditating before writing works for so many people. So, consider updating your journal after your daily psychic practices. Doing this is also a way to make sure you have relevant information to add to the journal.

A psychic journal is for you to record every step (and misstep) of your mediumship journey. By writing your experiences down, you can measure your progress. More importantly, it makes for easy analysis of the spiritual messages you receive.

As you get started on your mediumship journey, you may need extra help to boost your abilities. In that case, think about using pendulums, crystals, tarot cards, gemstones, or a Ouija board in your practices. These are all psychic tools that can amplify your psychic abilities and help you tune into them more quickly.

Chapter Four: Understanding Your Spiritual Body

"You don't have a soul. You are a Soul. You have a body."

−C. S. Lewis

In the last few chapters, I mentioned something called the "energy field." Well, this chapter is all about this field and the spiritual body. In spiritual settings, an energy field is called an aura.

Every individual and object in the universe emits energy. An aura is an electromagnetic field through which you channel spiritual energy, surrounding every living and non-living thing. Your aura is an invisible projection of your life force. Contrary to what many people think, it is not a single entity.

The aura comprises seven separate layers, all of which are interconnected. Together, these layers form a somewhat cohesive body. Thus, it might look like a less refined form of their physical body when you see the aura around someone. Each layer reflects one aspect of a person's life.

A person's aura is a sign of their energy. It has a lot of impact on their ability to connect with others. Typically, it extends about two to three feet from the body, but those who have experienced tragedy and trauma often have much broader auras, meaning that theirs may extend over three feet from their body.

The energy field is invisible, so most people don't see it around others. But those with the gift of clairvoyance can see, read, and interpret the aura. Being clairvoyant means you can see people's energy patterns, scenes, and blockages when looking at their aura.

When you meet a person, and you sense their "vibe," it is the emission of their personal energy you perceive. The aura is the channel through which you get specific information about people you don't know. It is the reason you can tell if someone is trustworthy or not. How you react to someone depends on the energy they radiate around you.

At this point, you are likely wondering what this has to do with your journey to mediumship. As I said, an aura is a projection or manifestation of a person's spiritual energy. You can tell a person's mental, emotional, spiritual, and even physical standing by reading their aura's colors. From the shape to the color and color shade, all aspects of the life force energy field are there for you to understand a person better.

As a medium, when you clairvoyantly see a ghost, you can also see its aura. Through this, you can detect valuable information about the spirit.

One of the auric field layers is the astral layer which you may call the spiritual layer. This layer is home to your celestial body, or if you prefer, your spiritual body. You cannot go to spiritual dimensions in your physical form because it is made of entirely different elements. To visit nonphysical dimensions, you need your astral body. Some people also call the astral form *the soul.*

When you start developing your mediumship ability, there will be plenty of situations when you need to go into a spiritual dimension yourself. It might be because you need to talk to a spirit, your spirit guide, or another higher-dimensional being. Regardless of the reason, you can only astral travel in your spiritual form. Therefore, understanding the aura's operations and the spiritual body can make all the difference for you.

Back to the layers of the aura, there are seven, as I said. Each layer has one solid color, which carries a lot of meaning, but it goes beyond that. Every layer is also connected to your seven energy centers, which are also known as the Chakras.

Individually, the auric layers vary in size and depth, and this is determined by an individual and the point they are in life. In a healthy individual, the aura usually has very bright colors. In contrast, dull colors are found in an unhealthy and weak aura. The size may also become small or large, depending on a person's quality of health. This means that no two people have the same auras.

The seven layers of your aura pulsate from your body. The first layer is the closest to your material form, while the 7th layer is the furthest. In retrospect, the seventh layer is the closest to your higher awareness. It has the highest vibrations because the further away a layer is from the physical body, the more vibration increases.

Some layers can be odd-numbered, while others are even-numbered. The odd-numbered layers have a defined structure, and they carry yang energy. In contrast, the even-numbered layers are more fluid, and they carry yin energy. Together, they culminate in a balanced and harmonization of your energy field.

The Seven Auric Layers

1. Etheric Layer: This layer is the closest to your material body. It is directly connected to the root chakra. With a bluish-grey color, you can easily see the etheric layer with your physical eyes.

2. Emotional Layer: After the subtle etheric body, the next is the emotional layer. It is the home of emotions and feelings. It is directly connected to the sacral chakra. In most people, this layer has all the colors of the rainbow. When you go through emotional stress, the colors turn murky and dark. You can tell someone's emotional state from reading this layer. It can also provide information on the state of the chakras.

3. Mental Layer: The mental layer is the third subtle energy body of the aura. It is linked to your solar plexus chakra. It indicates your cognitive processes and mental state, which makes it the seat of your thoughts. The standard color of this layer is bright yellow.

4. Astral Layer: When you hear of a spiritual cord connected to everything in the universe, the astral layer is the first thing that should come to mind. It is where you form the thread that connects you with every other being. This subtle body usually is bright pink with a rosy tint. And is connected to your heart chakra. You can get information about interpersonal relationships by reading the astral layer colors.

5. Etheric Template: An etheric template is a nonphysical form of your body. It contains the blueprint of your material body on the physical plane. Everything that happens on the physical level is recorded in your etheric template. The color may vary from person to person. The throat chakra is associated with this layer.

6. Celestial Layer: This is the sixth layer away from your physical body. It is linked to the third eye chakra. The celestial layer carries powerful vibrations, so the third eye is the seat of intuition. It is your connection to the Divine and all other higher-dimensional beings. This layer typically has a pearly white color.

7. Ketheric Template: The Ketheric template is about 3 feet from the body. It is the layer where you can become one with the universe. It contains every information about your previous lifetimes. Of all the auric layers, this one has the most potent and most powerful vibrations. It is connected to the crown chakra, with a golden color.

Your aura can change, depending on the events of your life. Still, most people always have two primary colors around them. Sometimes, an inauthentic color may even appear around a person's aura. That happens because of environmental issues or programming. For instance, being in a stressful relationship can add another color to your aura for the relationship duration.

Also, your emotional and physical experiences impact the colors in your aura. Suppose you have a severe case of acute pain. There, your aura's colors may change to reflect that. Having a hangover can also change your auric colors.

Despite all these, some colors usually are part of everyone's aura. These colors represent different things in different people, particularly when they appear with other colors. Interestingly, their meanings also change based on their tone and shade. A bright orange color in the auric field has a different interpretation from a dark orange color.

You must keep this information in mind when reading your aura or that of another person. Here are the most common colors in the aura and their respective meanings. Note these colors aren't in order, and they can appear in any of the seven subtle energy bodies.

• Yellow

Yellow means creativity, friendliness, and relaxation. You can find this in the aura of an individual who is curious and highly interesting. A yellow aura represents a busy mind. Someone with this aura color always has something going on in their head. To deal with this, you will find them immersing themselves in things such as baking, sewing, interior design, painting, and other practical forms of art. This color concentrates strongly on joy and is typically found around intelligent people.

• Green

Green in a person's aura indicates compassion, healing energy, divine wisdom, and a natural connection to Mother Earth. It is the color you find around the auras of energy healers. People of this color are innovative, logical, and visionary. They tend to live in their reality. They have a knack for solo activities due to their lone-wolf nature. A green aura means that the person is nurturing, social, and a great communicator.

• Red

Red in an aura symbolizes materialism. It is a color centered upon the material realm. Individuals with red in their auras like to think and do. They are strong and assertive, making them suitable for leadership positions. They are also risk-takers and are intrinsically motivated in life. They love to win, which is why this color is common among professional athletes and CEOs. Red-aura people also love intense activities.

• Purple

Conversely, auric purple represents intuition, creativity, and emotions. That explains why purple is the color of the third eye chakra, the intuition seat in the energy system. If you find purple in your aura, it means you take spiritual evolution seriously. It also indicates that you are gentle and spiritually enlightened.

- **Blue**

A blue aura can be called the complete opposite of a red aura. Just like red, blue represents compassion. But it also represents a tendency to shy away from the spotlight. People with this color in their aura are selfless by nature, which explains why it is common among teachers, nurses, caregivers, etc. Empaths typically have blue auras.

The above are the most common colors you would typically find in people's auras. Some people have more peachy colors, such as pink, orange, peach, in their field. Colors like these symbolize a sort of creativity quite peculiar. They also focus significantly on relationships, fun, and companionship. To people with peachy auras, family and friends are everything.

Knowing the meanings of the aura colors is not quite as important as seeing the aura itself. To read your aura, you need to learn how to see it first. Now, you can either perceive the aura through your clairvoyance or intuition.

For you or anyone else to sense or perceive the aura, some level of self-awareness is necessary. You must be perceptive enough to understand the end of the self and the beginning of another. Otherwise, your perception and interpretation of someone's aura may be your perception of them.

Put simply; you must develop the ability to see through yourself to see someone else's energy field. You have your energy field, meaning you perceive yours first before seeing other people's. If you don't learn to make a discernment, you may read your aura as that of another person.

If this happens, it can lead to you forming a wrong perception of the said person. Spiritual mediums take time to master the skill of bilocation (the ability to leave one's own body while remaining close to monitoring or perceiving the environment). With this skill, you can be adept at providing accurate aura interpretations.

How to See the Aura

Seeing your aura (or *any* aura) requires you to be in the right environment. Beginners need to have the right setting. Otherwise, you may keep practicing . . . achieving nothing tangible. A suitable background can make or mar your practice.

A plain-colored background is needed to see the vibrant colors of your energy field. So, try it in a room with a white wall or background. You may also use a backdrop. If you are trying to see your aura, you will need a mirror. In case you don't have one, you can try seeing the aura around your hand by placing it on a white piece of paper.

The environment you use should be quiet and comfortable. It should be a place where you can focus on the aura without being distracted or interrupted. Assuming you already have a part of your house designated for psychic exercises and practice, that room would be the perfect place to practice.

Furthermore, your location needs proper lighting. Low lighting can hinder your ability to perceive the energy field. The light in your room should be soft, without being too dark or too light. It should be the right amount. To avoid being strained or stressed, your eyes should be comfortable with the level of light. Natural light is ideal for aura practice, but you may use lamps or candles. Just make sure that you have the right concentration of light.

Once the environment is set for practice, you can go ahead by following the instructions below.

Seeing Someone Else's Aura

- Ask your subject to stand in front of a white wall. Make sure the individual already knows the details of what you will be doing. The subject should wear clothes that have no patterns because they can be distracting.

- Look directly at your subject. As you gaze, relax your sight. Stare at a specific spot for about 30 to 60 seconds. Focus on the spots in your peripheral vision, but make sure your eyes are a little out of focus. A hazy outline may appear to you around the edges. It should look transparent or look like white light. In a few minutes, this color may change to the aura's color.

It is best to practice by focusing on a small area. When trying to see someone else's aura, pick a specific part of their body, such as their head, to be your focal point. Suppose colors appear to you on your first try. There, try to determine the colors you see. Remember that the colors may be clear and bright, dark, cloudy, and muddy.

Note: you may follow the same steps to see your own aura. But stand in front of your mirror rather than against a white wall. Also, consider starting with just your hand when trying to see your aura. It makes the process easier for you.

Most beginners don't see more than one color on their first try. But in exceptional cases, some see several colors at once. The more you practice seeing auras, the more color variations you can see. It, of course, takes consistent practice.

You must be aware of after images when you try aura reading. After-images are usually the result of staring at one spot for a long time. They are the direct inverse of the object you are staring at, and they are not auras.

The difference is clear - after images tend to appear briefly in front of your eyes, regardless of where you look. The colors also appear in pairs - black and white, orange and blue, green and pink, yellow and violet.

Don't forget to record whatever you see in your journal. You can even draw instead of writing down. So, sketch out an outline and shade with the colors you see, using this for later analysis. You may show the drawing to your subject to let them know their aura's look.

The aura sometimes shows colors that are hard to reimagine or recreate artistically. If you see colors like that, try your best to get a close representation. Then, you can verbally describe whatever differences there are between your drawing and what you saw.

Cleansing Your Aura

Sometimes, the aura becomes toxic and murky because of the energy it picks up around. When this happens, the consequence is usually a disruption in the smooth running of the energy field. You must make sure your energy field is in optimal condition at all times. The best way to make sure this is to cleanse it regularly. Aura cleansing is a vital ritual that should be a part of your daily or weekly routine. A few useful techniques for cleansing the aura include:

- Meditation
- Visualization
- Positive affirmations
- Smudging, also known as burning sage,
- Energy healing
- Crystal healing

The exercises discussed in Chapter 3 can help with cleansing and balancing your aura.

Your spiritual body is just as important as your physical body. Taking care of your aura is your way of ensuring that your spiritual journey into mediumship progresses without hiccups getting in the way. Understanding your aura and developing awareness of other people's auras can take time. But if you dedicate yourself to the process, you will reap the benefits in time.

Perhaps the most critical thing with aura reading is that your ability to see an aura depends on your dominant psychic sense. If you are clairvoyant, you are more likely to see the aura with your physical eyes. Otherwise, you may sense or perceive it through intuition; how you see the aura does not matter. What matters is your interpretation of what you see.

Chapter Five: Preparation, Protection, and Intention

"Spirit can only communicate with us on our current level of understanding. Our spiritual habits determine what that level will be."

−Anthon St. Maarten

One of the most important things to remember when starting your mediumship journey is protection. Perhaps it is more important than any other thing. Going on a spiritual journey is no easy task, particularly for beginners. You don't know what to expect. The spiritual dimensions are not like the ones familiar to you already.

Connecting with spirit requires you to let go of control and submit yourself to your feelings to a reasonable extent. It is difficult for many. Plus, if you don't do it the right way, it might backfire. Whether you want to visit a spirit realm or channel a spirit to the material realm, preparing yourself for the experience is necessary.

Good preparation isn't just physical; you must also prepare spiritually. Meditating is one way you can prepare for the spiritual journey, but it is just a basic ritual. You have to do much more than meditating. Whether you are working by yourself or helped by a spirit guide or any other person, conducting a ritual cleansing is the first thing you do to prepare yourself.

Ritual cleansing is a symbolic way of getting rid of old and toxic energy to set an intention for your spiritual journey. Every day, you encounter negativity in the form of gossip, work stress, relationship breakups, and other things. All of these can cumulatively result in spiritual energy blockage if you allow them to gather power. Going on a spiritual journey with so many energy blockages can hinder you from achieving your goals.

The purpose of spiritual cleansing is to eliminate all the negativity from your spiritual body so you can be at the highest vibration possible. It is a way of reclaiming your power and preparing for what is to come.

To prepare yourself for spiritual cleansing, you need to take a bath. A bath, in this context, does not refer to your regular cleaning routine. You need to add bath salts to your bathwater. Salt is regarded as a traditional cleansing element. It is believed that one can use it to get rid of negative spirits and energy. Your bath water should be hot and steamy.

As you bath in the water, think of certain areas in your life that need to be rid of toxicity and negativity. Meditate on the things that seem to keep your energy stuck. Reflect on everything that needs to be released so you can clear your spirit.

Consider writing down everything that comes to mind. Put it all in a list. Then, visualize the negativity disappearing from your life in the form of clouds of dust going with the wind. In the process, chant a mantra that represents what you want to do. An example of a good mantra is "I release negative energy from my life and body. I release its hold over me. I reclaim my power. I reclaim the strength of my spirit."

After this, burn the paper on which you have the list. You may use a match, lighter, or candle to ignite the fire. Make sure to do it in a spot where you are unlikely to start a fire. A good place is in the bathroom, over your sink or bathtub. Put a plate beneath so you can get the ashes. Then, scatter them outside.

Recite "I am cleansed and freed by the flame. My spirit is purified" as the paper burns, and you scatter the ashes outside. As you recite, envision the negativity vaporizing from your spirit.

Once you have performed the ritual bath and cleansed yourself to prepare for your connection to the spiritual dimension, the next thing is to set your intention.

Many people underestimate the importance of intention setting in spiritual endeavors. They don't understand that it can make all the difference in their journey. Perhaps the reason is that most people confuse intention for goals. Setting an intention differs from setting goals for the spiritual connection you want to establish.

Some people think that letting go of control equals having no established objective for what you are doing. That is wrong. Having an intention is the key to staying grounded when you feel confused. It is like a raft - something you can hold on to while connected to the spiritual dimension.

It is normal to experience fleeting moments of confusion during a spiritual journey. You can't always navigate everything mentally. Trying to process it intellectually might make your head explode. But when you have an intention, you have no reason to worry because your mind will remain in the right place.

The question is, how do you set a definite intention that can act as your raft in the spiritual realm? Remember that the intention also has to be open-ended enough to encompass any kind of experience you have in the spiritual realm.

For one, you have to distinguish between your intentions and goals. Understand that they are two different things. From personal experience, I can affirm that using an intention is much better for enabling spiritual growth. Goals are fixated on particular outcomes you want to achieve before a specific period. They are typically black or white – it is either this or that. There is no in-between, but when you consider that you are dabbling in waters you have never been before, you will see why it is more reasonable to set an intention instead of setting goals.

Set the Intention

Setting the intention may appear like an easy task, but it requires you to put in work. First, you need to answer the question of what you want to know. What knowledge do you seek from the spirit world? You may need time to think about this to develop the best answer possible. You must be transparent when determining your intention.

Once you know your intention, you must work on being your best self for the trip ahead. One way I recommend is to incorporate a lot of spiritual activities into your daily routine. Start and end your day with meditation. Try inviting happy spirits from the other side through visualization. Make it a deliberate point to invite happy spirits when you make your intention. Also, work on improving your awareness by grounding yourself in the present regularly.

Some tips to help you set an excellent intention are:

- Word it as something you control.
- Put it in the present tense.
- Focus on the vibe you get from the intention. It should resonate and feel inspiring.
- Consider writing it down in your journal.
- Remember to keep it to yourself only.

While setting the intention, you must also raise your vibration. It is an integral part of your preparation. Of course, you already know that meditation is the best way to raise your vibrational level. But it is not the only way - spending time in nature, lighting scented candles, and decluttering are other ways you can do that. Listening to high vibrational music also helps. The essential thing is to do things that light you up on the inside. These things are different for everyone, so find what works for you.

Raising your vibration requires a lot of energy. But it is a crucial part of your preparation, so you cannot pass it up. As I mentioned before, spirits on the other side also have to reduce their vibration so you can communicate with them. Anything to the contrary will cause an imbalance.

Protecting Yourself

The spiritual realm is unpredictable, meaning that anything can happen to a medium while they are there. Not all spirits are festive. Some are malicious and toxic. Protecting yourself before you establish a connection with the spiritual realm is a must. No protection means leaving yourself vulnerable to unwanted entities.

Protecting yourself begins with having a strong assurance in yourself. The intention you set determines the efficacy of your protection. The time you use to create your protection should match your needs or goals.

Below, I have an exercise you can do once a day to build confidence and prepare for the spiritual dimension. The exercise involves creating a sort of protective shield around yourself. The purpose of this is to prevent yourself from attacking negative spirits or energies.

Visualization Exercise for Protection

• Envision a stream of pure white light entering your head from above. Let it fill your body until every part is covered. Imagine every grey-colored force in your system being transformed into white when the stream of light touches them.

• Once your entire body is filled with white light, allow it to radiate through your body and about 1 meter from your body. If done the right way, others can see the white light force around you in the shape of a nebula.

• Conclusively, picture a protective sphere-forming around the nebula to create a sort of protective envelope around your energy field.

If you could see the protection, it would look similar to an egg. You may even sense it physically surrounding you. The more you can sense it, the stronger it is, so its chances of being penetrated are meager.

I recommend doing this exercise every morning and evening to enter your force completely.

Naturally, there are plenty of other things that can help you prepare effectively for your spiritual voyage. For a start, consider using appropriate trigger items to engage the spirit you are channeling. That means you have to do some research on the spirit before the D-day. Using items associated with spirits while they were alive is suitable to invoke responses and interactions. If you have anything linking you to the spirit, talk about it out loud. It will help pique the spirit's interest so he or she can interact with you.

Acting the role of an ally or caring observer can help you form a closer connection with spirits, resulting in a more wholesome experience. But this requires you to protect yourself. Otherwise, you might end up with an undesired attachment. Bringing forth a spirit is one thing but being haunted or stalked by ghosts is a different ball game entirely. You have to be careful.

Once you can sense, hear, or see a spirit or another otherworldly entity, communicate with respect and empathy. It does not matter whether the spirit is talking to you or through you. Mutual respect is necessary. If you don't understand a message, you have the option of requesting clarity.

Do nothing that could feel like a threat or provocation to the spirit. Ghost hunters typically use provocative methods, but as a medium, you shouldn't. You might end up with a hurt or angry spirit seeking revenge. Be firm and polite in your interactions.

Again, trust your instincts. If your instincts tell you that a situation cannot be handled or contained, then leave. That is another reason protection is essential. There are lots of ways besides the protection technique explained earlier. You can carry protective crystals and gemstones, wear a pentagram or crucifix, and do a ritual before you leave.

A stated earlier, some messages may not be clear to you but always trust what you hear. If you hear nothing, then ask the spirit to clarify. Doubt scares spirits away; it's good to keep any manifestation of doubt away. Judge properly.

Before trying to channel a real spirit, try testing yourself first. Do this alone or with friends. Get a mirror, meditate in front of the mirror, and try to induce a trance. Fortunately, this is something you can do anywhere. It is an excellent way of teaching yourself to be open to spirit.

Go for a place where you sense intense spiritual energies. Observe any messages, sensations, or impressions. Afterward, research and crosscheck the accuracy of your channeling and reading session. Remember that the results of your test may differ from the actual thing. After all, a lived experience differs significantly from an imagined or imitated one.

Other ways to prepare for your spiritual trance include:

- **Don't Smudge**: Smudging means burning sage - an ancient herb for cleansing rituals. It is typically the foundation of rituals and spells, but it is not for spirits. The purpose of sage is to keep ghosts and spirits away, whether bad or good. Using sage before a session is your way of telling ghosts to stay away from you. If you smudge before attempting the communication, the spirit would likely be cranky and ill-mannered.

- **Set Up Multiple Conduits**: The point of conduits is to help the ghosts deliver messages. Spirits need conductors sometimes. As you prepare to contact the dead, set up different conduits within the venue. Throughout history, spirits have been recorded as communicating through a liquid, candle flames, and scent. You may also set up audio-visual recording devices since they are known to be useful as well.

- **Embrace Death**: Embracing death is a way of celebrating life. Remember that I said there is nothing like death. We grow up with a fear of ghosts thanks to the horror movies we watched. In reality, you will see that your fear of ghosts reflects your relationship with mortality. Accepting the actuality of death is difficult - the experience is scary, painful, and heartbreaking. Connecting with the spiritual realm is an opportunity for you to explore your own physical realm's impertinence. In the end, you will realize that a robust and beautiful soul results from "death."

I want to conclude this chapter by emphasizing that creating a bridge between the physical and spirit realms requires you to develop a language between spirit and yourself. It will be your way of "talking" to spirit. Doing this means paying attention to the signs around you.

That brings me to the three clairs most important to psychics: clairvoyance, clairsentience, and clairaudience. These allow you to see, hear and feel when forming your connection with the other side. They are the most common channels through which spirit initiates communication with humans. As you work on developing a shared language with spirit, you will experience more and more signs. Pay attention to them all!

The next three chapters focus on the three clairs as stated above. Discover more about their pivotal importance in your spiritual mediumship development.

Chapter Six: Psychic Abilities I: Clairsentience

"People high in the psychic gift of clairsentience are some of the sweetest people you will ever meet."

—Catherine Corrigan

Clairsentience is a prominent psychic ability that mediums tend to have. As defined in an earlier chapter, it is the gift of "clear feeling." It is the ability to feel and experience people's emotions precisely as if they were yours. Interestingly, clairsentience is not a widely known ability. You don't see it portrayed in movies and TV shows like other psychic senses.

When people think about psychic abilities, they think more about clairvoyance and clairaudience. As a result, most people don't even realize when having psychic experiences connected with their clairsentience ability.

A clairsentient psychic can receive psychic information, messages, and impressions via emotions, feelings, and physical sensations. To put it simply, perhaps it is about receiving intuitive hits through sensing. Being a clairsentient psychic means you get gut feelings about people and objects alike, *even places.* You can receive intuitive impressions from anything that emits energy.

An example of clairsentience is if you pass by a homeless shelter and feel pangs of hunger. Or if you hug your friend and feel incredibly happy or sad, depending on their emotion. Your clairsentience may even reflect when watching movies or news stories. Seeing reports on violent crimes may move you to tears. If you can relate to one or more of these examples, you may just be clairsentient.

Here are other signs that can help you discover whether clairsentience is your dominant psychic ability.

- You can feel someone else's physical or emotional pain.

- You cannot withstand being in crowds due to the influx of feelings.

- You get physically and emotionally drained when you spend time with people.

- Your instincts about people, places, and situations are usually correct.

- You can't stand cluttered or messy home or workspace because it makes you feel stressed.

- You get waves of emotions from nowhere

These are some of the most common signs experienced by clairsentient psychics. Check if any of these apply to you. If your friends have always said you are emotional or too sentimental, that could be another indication.

I stated earlier that everyone has all psychic abilities, but we all tend to tilt toward one or more abilities more than the others. Mediums tilt toward clairsentience, clairvoyance, and clairaudience because they are the senses through which spirits communicate. It does not mean they do not or cannot communicate through the other psychic senses; they prefer these three over the other.

Developing your clairsentience is vital to be in-tune with your intuition. Before I get there, you may wonder how constantly soaking in feelings, emotions, and energies feels.

Yes, being clairsentient is akin to being a sponge. But that is if you don't learn to control your ability. Learning to manage your ability is necessary. If you don't, you will always find yourself stuck with unwanted emotions and energies. You must also know how to respond to the intuitive hits you get.

The only way to do this is to practice knowing when you have a clairsentient hit and, more important, managing your psychic senses. Once you master this, you won't feel drained of energy. And you can use your ability to further your interest in mediumship. Quickly at all, you will start accessing clear and prompt psychic messages.

Now that you understand that clairsentience isn't a bad thing if you manage it in the right way, here's what a clairsentience experience might feel like to you.

- **Emotional Feelings:** Clairsentient psychics often receive messages through emotions. For example, you may mirror your partner's anxiety over a scheduled visit to the doctor.

- **Physical Sensations**: Another way you may get clairsentient experiences is through sensations in the physical body. A good example is feeling pangs of hunger when you pass by a homeless shelter.

When you mirror the sensation, it does not mean you are hungry as well. It usually doesn't last beyond a few minutes. It often happens when you connect with spirits. If the spirit passed from a physical condition, you might get a tingling sensation in that part of your body as well. It is usually brief, and it is not scary.

Managing clairsentience is essential, yet it seems hard. With nothing to guide their way, people stay indoors because they fear getting drained when they spend time among people. Feeling the energy from people, places, and objects gets draining, which makes control necessary.

If you can't manage clairsentience, you may learn to shy away from parties or become a social recluse in the worst scenario. That does not have to happen. As I said, you can learn to manage your clairsentient hits. Only those who haven't mastered their gift experience overwhelming feelings from others.

However, there are ways you can develop and master your clairsentience ability. Don't forget that mastering it is the key to managing it.

Focus on Your Environment

Clairsentient psychics are extra conscious and super sensitive to their immediate environment. They simply can't miss a thing. They will notice if someone moves their favorite flower vase an inch. That is how incredibly aware they are. It is one thing you can use to your advantage. You can develop your clairsentience by focusing on your surroundings.

How does your environment look? Is the space cluttered? Do the dirty dishes make you feel anxious? Well, clutter in your home can invoke a lot of feelings. But that is not the point. You have to create a specific space in your home that isn't like the others. This space will be your psychic development area. It should be clean and fresh with a sacred ambiance. More than once, I have mentioned the importance of having space solely for psychic reasons.

Choose a spot like the corner of your room or, if you can, a whole room you can use for psychic things. Add everything, such as your meditation mat or chair, journal, blanket, crystals, and other psychic tools, in that space. Put anything else that makes you happy and is crucial to your psychic journey into this space. Add nothing that could be needlessly distracting from the purpose of the sacred space.

Clairsentience heightens sensitivity, so it helps to design your psychic space, making sensitivity feel good. The key to this is to go green. Greenery makes you feel calm, which is how you should always feel when you are in psychic mode. It makes you feel grounded and connected to nature. Besides having a green scenery, consider using organic cleaning products made from plants and essential oils. They are amazing.

Use sage to clear up space. Yes, sage is used to tell spirits to stay away, but that only if you burn it right before going into a trance. Here, you have to set an intention for the sage to keep negativity and darkness away. Set an intention for love and light to fill up your space before smudging.

Doing all the above can make a significant difference in how clairsentience affects you and how you respond to it. Now that you have set up the right space for clairsentience (and other psychic practices), get to the actual exercises for developing your ability.

Use Photos to Develop Clairsentience

The photo technique is a fun exercise I love doing. The best thing about it is that you might do even better than you expect. Just make sure you feel free and relaxed before you try it. You need a photo of someone you have no information about. You should have never met that person before. Don't use the picture of your favorite celebrity even if you have never met them. Celebrities have enough information about their lives on the internet. Instead, you can ask your friend to show you a photo of a family member you don't know. Your friend should know the person well so they can help corroborate the information you get.

• Hold the photo in your two hands. Look at the person's face and focus specifically on their eyes. Envision their feelings from the picture. How did they feel when the picture was taken? Happy? Sad? Anxious? Enthusiastic? Do they seem trustworthy? Allow yourself to imagine and go with the flow.

• Focus for a few minutes until you have the information you want. When you are done, deliberate on it for a few more minutes, then relay it to your friend. Ask them for feedback.

Repeat this clairsentient exercise at least twice every week with different photos all the time. Consistency will allow you to build your clairsentience and confidence.

Try Psychometry

Psychometry is the practice of reading the energy of an object. When you touch something, you leave an energetic imprint on that item. Your favorite sweatshirt, toy, and necklace all hold an imprint of your energy. We all unknowingly transfer energy to objects, usually those that we own. The more you use or love the item, the more energy you leave on it. Before you know it, you have accumulated energy. That is precisely why psychometry is useful for developing clairsentience.

By reading the energy of an object, you can get enough information about the object's owner. It is best to practice psychometry on an object you do not own. You already know everything about yourself, so there is no point in that. Ask your best friend to come over with a piece of jewelry owned by someone in their family or anything else that is a family heirloom. Jewelry is the best because metal retains energy better than other elements. Again, the owner of the item should be someone you don't know.

• Rub your palms together for a few seconds. Do a quick breathing exercise, then hold the object in your hand. Don't do anything for a couple of minutes. Just hold on to the object.

- Sense the energy radiating from the object. Is it negative or positive? Determine what kind of energy it is.

- Feel the owner's energy. What can you sense? Try to get as much information as you can from the energy you sense. Several sensations can come to you about the history of the item and its owner.

As usual, let your friend corroborate whatever information you receive from the item. When you practice psychometry consistently, you can read an object's energy without touching or holding it.

Form a Crystal Grid

Crystals enhance psychic abilities, which makes having them around a great thing for mediums. My favorite thing about using crystals for psychic development is that they require little to no effort. Crystals such as amethyst and fluorite support all psychic abilities, but they are great for clairsentience in particular. You can make crystal grids effortlessly. They take just a few minutes, and the possibilities of mistakes are nonexistent.

- Buy 12 crystals. Choose crystals that feel connected to you. You can get more than 12. You may buy 12 of one crystal or mix them up. I recommend buying a mix of amethyst and fluorite.

- Place a crystal in the center and arrange the remaining around it to form a circle.

- While setting the crystals in place, set the intention to enhance your clairsentience ability. Make it Clair, or clear, that you want to receive psychic messages through clairsentient hits.

- Place the crystal grid in your sacred psychic space or under your bed.

- That's all!

To boost your crystals' powers, you may rub essential oils on them before you form the grid.

Don't forget that meditation is essential in all you do, psychic-wise. Make meditation a part of your clairsentience development exercises. Follow the instructions for traditional meditation but set the intention to connect with your intuitive ability.

You can develop clairsentience. Anyone can develop clairsentience. Follow all the tips in this chapter, and you will master your gift in time. Remember that you learn at your own pace, so don't be too anxious to learn in no time.

Chapter Seven: Psychic Abilities II: Clairaudience

"Intuition goes before you, showing you the way. Emotion follows behind to let you know when you go astray. Listen to your inner voice. It is the calling of your inner voice. It is the calling of your spiritual GPS seeking to keep you on track towards your true destiny."

−Anthon St. Maarten

Clairaudience is another psychic ability dominant in mediums. It is possibly the second most-known ability after clairvoyance. As you already know, it is the gift of psychic hearing. When you start your psychic development journey, you will find that some skills are more comfortable to master than others. Fortunately, clairaudience is one of those that is easiest to develop. But what is clairaudience?

It is a psychic ability or sense that allows you to receive psychic impressions, messages, and information via hearing. You might get them in the form of voices, words, sounds, or music. The good thing is the experience is neither creepy nor scary. You hear everything in your head as if you were thinking out aloud. Sometimes, you might even hear with your physical ears. But remember, spirits on the other side are no longer in a material form – therefore, they need not communicate with a physical voice.

Clairaudient psychics usually receive intuitive messages in five different ways. You may have experienced some of these before.

The first way is to hear your voice aloud in your head. The voice is usually soft and subtle, and it may sound like you have an internal monologue. If you are doing a mediumship reading and the connected spirit communicates via clairaudience, you won't hear the voice they had when they were on Earth. Instead, you hear the spirit in your voice, inside your head. It is like communicating telepathically. As you develop your ability, you will learn to differentiate between your voice and spirit.

A second way that clairaudient messages may be received is via sounds. These sounds always have a symbolic or literal meaning you can interpret. If a spirit wants to tell you something, it might communicate via music. For example, you might hear a birthday-themed song if they recently had their birthday.

On relatively rare occasions, spirits communicate via physical sounds from your normal hearing. This rarely happens. You might hear sounds, words, or music without a recognized source. The sound is usually ethereal and beautiful. It may leave you feeling enchanted.

Another way spirits communicate is via their ethereal voice. Established mediums can hear the voice of the spirit telepathically. When this happens, you will hear the voice precisely as it was when they were alive. It tends to happen with spirits you are already familiar with—for example, the spirit of your grandfather or deceased uncle.

Last, spirits communicate via distress warnings. Experiences like this may be scary, which is why spirits only use this method when it is incredibly urgent. Clairaudient warnings often sound out loudly in your head. For example, you might hear a sudden "STOP" in your head as you are about to drive onto the highway. You might be startled, but it often turns out to be for a good cause.

Clairaudient experiences are easy to pass off as "It's all in your head," which many people do when they can't explain the voice source in their head. Understanding what clairaudient messages come from and how it feels to have the experience can provide insight into the events you have dismissed as "just in my head" in the past.

No psychic can deny this psychic ability has a dramatic flair, but it is not as dramatic as many believe. It is often very subtle – enough to dismiss without a second thought. How do you know when you have a clairaudient experience instead of regular thinking?

Knowing what to look for is vital. When you think of clairaudience, think of telepathy because it revolves around that. After all, telepathy is mind-to-mind communication that takes place without the use of any known sensory channels. When spirit drops a message in your head, they are communicating telepathically.

Clairaudience is like receiving a call from your cellphone without actually picking it up. Here are some things to help you recognize the experience:

- It sounds like you are reading or thinking to yourself. It is like when reading alone by yourself. You can "hear" what you are reading in your head.
- The hearing is always internal but may be external on the rarest occasions.
- It is always for a good reason.
- It does not take away your free will. You can make your own choice.
- Sometimes appear like auditory impressions. Thoughts may "pop" into your head out of nowhere.
- Typically, brief and straight to the point.

Clairaudient messages come from the Divine, your spiritual team, and spirits on the other side. At first, you may not be able to tell the source of the psychic messages you receive. But, in time, you will start to get an idea or sense of who the message's sender is and why.

If the gift of clairaudience is your dominant psychic ability, then spirits will send you messages via clairaudient channels most times. However, how can you tell if you are a clairaudient psychic? There are many signs to observe.

• You often hear your name when no one is around you. If this happens to you regularly, it is an indicator you have the ability. Psychic hearing allows you to hear things that other people don't.

• Sensitivity to noise is a good sign of clairaudience. You may feel irritable, tired, or stressed when you are in an environment with too much noise. It is even more frustrating when people around you can't understand your sensitivity. So, you seek quiet and solitude. Consider getting headphones with noise-canceling technology to manage this sensitivity.

• Talking to yourself is another sign. Clairaudience pushes you to have conversations in your head most or all the time. You may find you are customarily distracted from interactions because you are immersed in your head.

• You enjoy music because it connects you to your soul. Clairaudient people often find music uplifting. Listening to music is an excellent way to raise your vibration and reconnect to your spirit. You may even have a music talent.

There are many other signs, but most clairaudient psychics often experience some or all the signs above. Think back on which of these you are familiar with and use your answer to determine if a psychic hearing is your prominent ability.

Whether you can relate to most of the signs discussed or not, psychic hearing is crucial to your mediumship journey. Therefore, you must learn to develop it regardless. The good thing is clairaudience is relatively easy to develop. All you need is practice and a genuine desire to learn.

Think about your car or home radio. It has inbuilt stations, right? Any time you want to hear a station, you just have to tune in clearly, and you will hear everything they have. Clairaudience is just the same, with an almost imperceptible difference. The difference is in the subtlety of hearing. In this case, you are the radio. To develop psychic hearing, you have to tune into yourself. Developing psychic hearing is practically about learning how to tune inside and always receive clear messages.

Let's discuss ways you can develop your psychic hearing skills.

Train Yourself to Pick up Astral Sounds

For starters, you need to practice the sensitization of your hearing. It is simple yet effective. It works because training your regular hearing makes it easier to pick up nonphysical sounds from the spirit world.

A physical plane is generally a noisy place that has trained us to filter noise before it can alert our consciousness. But you can use the noisy environment to your advantage. That is where sensitization comes in. Here is an exercise to this effect.

- Find a safe space for this exercise. Take some deep breaths to ground yourself.

- Set an intention you want to enhance your gift of psychic hearing.

- Relax and focus on your hearing. At that moment, let it be your dominant sense.

- Gently allow yourself to tune into your environment. Focus on sounds that you rarely give attention to. Identify what you can hear. Perhaps a wind traveling through the trees behind your house or birds chirping.

Do this exercise every day but use different locations for each practice. See how much you can hear with each try. As you progress, put in more effort by stretching yourself in different directions with a different focus.

Musical Exercise

The point of this exercise is to help you detect and differentiate between subtle sounds. Practicing it can train you to discern between your thoughts and clairaudient messages. This exercise is quite an interesting one, so you might even have fun while at it. Try using music with heavy instrumentals. It helps to use band music. But classical music is also an excellent choice for training.

- Play your chosen band music and get into the groove. Submit to the jam.

- Now, focus on one instrument you can hear in the music. Yes, they are playing in harmony simultaneously, but you can single one out and focus on it. Isolate its sound from the remaining instruments.

One by one, isolate all the playing instruments' sounds until you have covered them all. With practice, you will get to that stage where you can cut off one of the sounds away until you can't hear the rest. Try this exercise two to three times weekly with different music.

"Visualize" Sound

Visualization is a visual technique, so how can you possibly "visualize" sound? Well, this exercise does not involve envisioning. The purpose is to improve your ability to hear messages communicated telepathically.

Can you imagine music playing in your head, almost as if you were using an actual music player? You need to do that alone in a still and quiet room where there are no other sounds. It is a beautiful way to develop clairaudience overall. Don't just stop at music. Try to imagine other sounds.

Envision all the sounds you were familiar with while growing up. Imagining sounds in your mind is a straightforward method to enhance your psychic hearing. Visualize your favorite artiste singing out in your mind as if you were in their concert.

Request for Spirit Messages

This trains you to have two-way conversations with spirit. It is a foolproof method for building confidence in your psychic hearing abilities. You can ask spirit for information – they need not come to you first. Practice requesting and receiving messages from higher-dimensional beings. In this context, spirit refers to your spiritual guides, not those on the other side. It also refers to Ascended Masters and your Higher Self.

Before you make any decision, ask your spirit guides for guidance. Then, wait for an answer to come. The answer can come in any form. Having two-way conversations with your spiritual team can advance your spiritual journey by a whole lot, particularly as an intending medium. It will also help you master the art of detecting spirit subtlety.

The most important thing with all your clairaudience exercises is to have fun while you are practicing them. That is important. Don't make it feel like a job or a task that you have to complete at a specific time. Have fun and allow yourself to go with the flow.

Note: Sometimes, clairaudience may be hard to develop. You might practice and practice without making headway in your development goals. If this happens, it could mean that your throat chakra is blocked. The psychic portal for clairaudience is directly connected to the throat chakra. Thus, blockage there hinders your ability to tune into your psychic hearing. If this happens to you, use your crystal grid to unblock it and get back in action.

Chapter Eight: Psychic Abilities III: Clairvoyance

"After years in utter darkness, I force my eyes into the light. For I must retain my sight, that I might view the wholeness of the void, objectively."

−Justin K. McFarlane Beau

Clairvoyance is the most known psychic ability. It is no wonder why some people use it synonymously with the word "psychic." It is widely portrayed in movies and TV shows as an over-the-top ability. Dramatic exaggeration is one reason it is widely misconceived. The extent of misconception is due to familiarity.

As you have learned, clairvoyance translates to "clear seeing." It is the ability to receive psychic or intuitive information via images, symbols, and visions. The "seeing" in clairvoyance happens in your mind's eye, which you already know as the third eye. So, don't expect to physically see a spirit lounging around in your home, waiting for you to get back from work. That is not how this gift works.

Suppose you are clairvoyant. In that case, you have likely noticed:

- Flashes of light and color around the corner of your eyes.

- Random images that disappear as fast as they appear, almost like a "flash."
- Movement out of your peripheral vision even when there is nobody else in a room with you.
- Vivid dreams that feel real enough.

Let's discuss these signs briefly so you can understand how they appear to you.

- **Visual Psychic Flashes**: Being clairvoyant means that you get flashes of light and color vision. It may be your spiritual team trying to get your attention or tell you something. For instance, you may see floating orbs of light, auras, glittering lights, twinkling lights, and shadows around the corner of your eyes.

- **Daydreams**: Psychic seeing concerns sight; therefore, visualization is a significant part of the ability. If you are clairvoyant, envisioning will come quickly to you. You can easily picture something in your mind because you see how it should all fit together.

- **Good with Direction**: Have you ever been to a location once, and it becomes imprinted in your mind? Do people describe you as a human GPS tracker? If you can relate to these, you are likely a clairvoyant psychic. It also means you are proficient at solving puzzles, reading maps, and completing mazes.

- **Vivid Imagination**: This links back with the previous sign. If you've been told that you have a very vivid imagination, it could be a manifestation of your psychic ability.

Without realizing it, you have probably experienced signs of clairvoyance all your life. The good thing is that you can pay more attention to clairvoyant signs once you know what to look for in yourself.

Even if you are already self-aware of your abilities, sometimes, feelings of doubt set in. Doubt is a recurring emotion when you begin your psychic journey. We all experience doubt at first.

One day, you are confident that everything you are experiencing is real. You feel attuned to your soul. You are amazed by the things you can do, and you enjoy sending love and light out to the universe. Another day, you feel doubt. "Do I have this ability?" "Can I communicate with spirits? Maybe it is all in my head." Or "I don't think I am made for this."

Questions like these are bound to arise, but it is up to you not to give in to them. Being a clairvoyant is tough, especially when everyone around you thinks it is a fluke and you are just wasting your time. You must avoid giving in to the feelings of doubt you experience by learning to trust your experience.

First, you must have faith in your personal experiences. Negative self-talk does not help. It causes blockage in your spiritual system. Then, you must turn to your spirit guides for signs. Even if you have never connected with any member of your spiritual team, they are waiting for you to seek their guidance. You can ask for signs at any time because they serve as reassurance.

Sometimes, you might receive messages that seem outrightly weird. It might push you to doubt your guides, but don't do it. Having trust in your spirit guides is not an option; it is a must. Your guides always send the right messages. It is up to you to interpret in the right way. Interpreting messages from spirit guides does take some practice. Symbols and metaphors are notably harder to interpret. Understand that you are taking baby steps. Don't judge yourself or feel bad about it.

In the movies, clairvoyant psychics often see the future precisely as it is going to happen. Most of the time, they get a frightening caption attached to it. But in reality, clairvoyant hits are less dramatic and more subtle. Spirits love subtlety, meaning you should learn to expect subtle messages.

Below are the ways that you might receive clairvoyant messages:

• **Third Eye:** Clairvoyant messages are not physically visible – if you have the ability, you can only "see" with your mind's eye. The third eye chakra makes this possible. It is the channel through which messages from the spiritual dimensions are sent to this plane.

• **Images and Movies:** Another way clairvoyant messages appear is in an image snapshot or a movie scene. You might feel like there is a TV screen open in your mind where a movie is playing. All of these, of course, happen in your head. Some also appear as visions. For example, you might receive a vision of one symbol representing something you are familiar with – like a ring to symbolize "marriage."

• **Symbols:** It is vital to talk about symbols separately because they are critical to psychic messages. There are lots of times when you receive symbols instead of something you can easily interpret. Spirit guides send symbols so you can work on interpretation. For instance, you may see images of a baby crib in your trance. It could mean that your subject is about to experience the birth of a child. If you cannot decipher the symbols immediately, don't fret. Just take your time until you crack them. Over time, you can even work with your spirit guides to decipher the literal meanings of received symbols.

Developing clairvoyance is easily one of the most fun things to do. Like everything else discussed so far, you only need to be dedicated to the practice. The learning process can be exciting. But don't forget to be kind to yourself. Even if you see no progress, ensure you keep practicing till you get it right. You will eventually get the hang out of it.

Numbers Visualization

As a clairvoyant, visualization is your stronghold. You can train yourself to become a super visualizer in time. The more you hone the skill, the more comfortable you will find using it. Remember that your third eye is responsible for psychic seeing. Therefore, these exercises are centered upon the third eye. That means you will practice seeing the pictures, symbols, and visions in your head.

Keeping your third eye chakra open is the key to receiving clairvoyant messages. That is why you must open your third eye first. Understand that the third eye chakra cannot be opened on the first try. Naturally, it requires you to put in several sessions. A few minutes of visualization practice every day can jumpstart your psychic seeing ability.

To visualize with numbers:

- Close your eyes. Perform a quick breathing exercise.
- Picture the number one in your head. Hold on to the picture for at least 10 seconds.
- If you can successfully do that, move on to the next number, which is two.
- Keep imagining until you get all the way to number ten.

Try this exercise for five to ten minutes every day—the more consistent, the better.

Clairvoyance Game

This game is played with a pack of Zener cards. These cards have different shapes, ranging from stars to circles and squares. They are fun for practicing clairvoyance, usually with a partner. You can order a pack on Amazon or check your local store. You can also make these cards on your own. Just get some index cards and draw different shapes on them. The shapes should include a circle, wavy lines, a star, a square, and a plus sign.

- Sit across from your partner or in separate chairs with your backs to each other.

- Grab one card, but don't let your partner see it. Let's assume you chose the circle card.

- Concentrate on seeing the circle with your third eye. Once the image has formed in your head, send it to your game partner telepathically.

- Next, let your partner know that you have sent the image, then ask them to reveal the image they received.

- Switch places with your partner – become the receiver while they send.

- Repeat the first few steps as explained

You can keep switching places for as long as you want. To make it more fun, try doing this exercise over the phone.

Crystals

As mentioned in the chapter about clairsentience, crystals are super incredible for developing psychic abilities. They are great for opening the third eye chakra. You can keep them in your psychic space or put them under your pillow when you go to bed. They are portable, which is why you can also carry them around with you. I recommend carrying them around because it is a constant reminder of your intention to work on your psychic abilities every day. Plus, they are pretty. Amethyst and fluorite help to open the third eye just as they can increase your psychic ability.

Dream Journal

Remember I said that vivid dreams are signs of clairvoyance. When you have vivid dreams, you shouldn't just let them go. Recording the dreams is essential. Sometimes, spirits send messages through the dream portal. Writing down your dreams and analyzing them can help you decipher such messages. When you sleep, your subconscious mind is the one in full charge of your body. That allows you to accept spiritual guidance more freely without your logical mind interfering. Your logical mind is why you would usually overlook or ignore psychic messages.

Sleep with your journal by your side. That way, you can write down your dreams when you are awake. After some days, weeks, or months, you may notice symbols and patterns that hold meaning. These symbols can remind you of an experience or something about another person.

Perhaps the best reason you should keep a dream journal is to help you understand how your ability is evolving. There is nothing more inspiring and motivating than seeing your progress. It helps you appreciate the effort you put in more.

Meditation to Open the Third Eye

Traditional meditation can help develop your psychic seeing ability. However, some meditations are specifically targeted at the third eye. They are much more effective and faster for someone on a psychic development path. The third eye can help you see mental blockages, energies, and other experiences in its full force and capacity.

As I said, you may be wondering why the third eye is not already opened. The third eye mostly stays closed and dormant. Unless you work actively toward opening it, it might never open – which explains why many people are not aware of their abilities. While third eye opening can help, learning to open and close your third eye at will is crucial. Otherwise, you will leave your psychic portal open to all kinds of intuitive hits. Not regulating when, how, and where you receive psychic hits can disrupt your life to an alarming extent.

Like other meditation types, third eye meditation should be done in a quiet and calm environment to benefit from the soothing vibes.

- Sit comfortably on the floor or a chair. Keep your spine upright, shoulders relaxed, and palms on your knees. Release the tension from your stomach, jaw, and face. Every part of your body should feel relaxed and be open to the incoming energy.

- Join your thumb and index fingers together as you close your eyes gently. Breathe in slowly and breathe out through your nose. With your physical eyes still closed, look up at the location of your third eye. You may also use your fingers to pinpoint the exact location.

- Allow your gaze to relax as you focus on your third eye. Keep breathing slowly until a white light appears. Let the white light spread and surround you.

- Enter a transcendental state of energy healing as the light surrounds you. Your focus will be at the highest and most powerful level.

- Release every lousy thought, feeling, and energy from your field. Just concentrate on improving the potentials of your third eye chakra.

Remain in this position for up to 20 minutes at a stretch. Playing relaxing music in the background can further help improve your focus. After 20 minutes, end the meditative session by bringing your palms to your heart and rubbing them together. After opening your eyes, sit for some minutes before you stand and get back to your routine.

This meditation exercise can be repeated every day until you are confident that your third eye is sufficiently open.

Below is another simple exercise for the third eye:

- Sit in the usual position
- Set the intention to open your third eye and improve your clairvoyant abilities
- Focus on the area where your third eye is located
- Visualize the chakra in a beautiful purple color, majestically spinning as it opens wider and wider

You may experience tingling between your eyebrows when you perform these exercises. It means that your third eye is opening. Be happy because it is a sign you will flourish with your clairvoyant gifts.

Now that you know how to master the three psychic abilities that will define your journey as a medium, let's contact the spirit world. It promises to be fun!

Chapter Nine: Contacting the Spirit World

"Think the thought,

See the image,

Develop a feeling,

Respond with the body,

Produce the results."

—James E. Melton

The time to contact the spirit world has come. The question is, how do you go about it? Everything you have been learning so far is a buildup to this. If you follow everything you have learned throughout the book correctly, contacting the spirit world will be like calling briefly at your best friend's house.

Forget everything you believe you know. Even if you have seen an otherworldly being before, this is different. Channeling spirits or establishing communication with the spirit world feels more real and intense when you are in the middle of it. Feeling spirits is fleeting and spontaneous. However, this is a deliberate action, which requires you to be in the best possible state.

I have explained the process of preparation for contacting the spirit world. As explained, you have to set the intention and protect yourself against unseen forces and spirits. Before you establish the connection, double-check to ensure that your protection is intact and functional. Set the intention firmly and clearly.

Here is a rundown of the steps involved in preparing yourself:

- Meditate to clear your mind and raise your vibration
- Do the protection exercise to form a protective shell around yourself
- Set the intention

Your intuition must be at the highest level possible, while your spiritual energy must be robust. Since this would likely be your first time contacting a spirit, consider calling a familiar spirit. An example is a family member or friend who has passed on to the other side. In time, you may contact spirits not directly linked or connected to you.

In a spiritual setting, the process of establishing communication with an otherworldly being is often called a séance. However, going by the literal meaning of a séance, it must be done by at least eight people. Also, a séance entails the invoked spirit using the medium as a vehicle.

Do not allow yourself to be possessed by any spirit – familiar or not – on your first practice. Besides the fact that it takes a lot of vital energy, it is also potentially dangerous. This chapter will explain two useful techniques for contacting the spiritual realm. The first is a formal technique for connecting with spirit, while the second is a method called mirror gazing.

There are so many rules to remember if you want your séance to succeed. These rules may seem too much, but they are vital for your safety. Following the correct framework is the key to getting it right. Understandably, you may miss a few things the first time. But, in time, the rules and steps will become second nature. When you get to that point, you will have a relatively smooth experience than you did your first time.

Here are the rules:

• Do not be skeptical about the experience you are about to have. Skepticism attracts negative energy, which frightens spirits away. Even when the spirit appears, it can block and affect communication. Have faith in yourself and your ability.

• Leave the invoked spirit alone if they don't initiate contact. If they show any sign of resistance, allow them to return. Do not bother spirit. They will inform you if they do have any message for you.

• Avoid channeling spirits just for curiosity. Do not do this for fun – it is not meant for your entertainment or amusement. Initiate contact only if you have questions to ask. Prepare your questions before connecting them. Be constructive with the questions.

• Accept the answers you receive without questioning the spirit. Even when it does not make sense to you at first, you will later decipher the meaning. Meanwhile, receive the answers.

• Spirits form attachments quickly. Do not be frightened if the spirit tries to touch or talk to you. But never should you touch the entity first – not unless they signal it is okay.

• Do not fabricate or stretching the information you receive. As people say on Twitter, don't "reach." In this context, reaching means going to an outrageous degree to force a specific meaning out of the situation. Avoid making personal observations, no matter how tempting.

• Do not lead people on with the information you receive. Avoid relying on incomplete information that can be interpreted in different ways. If you need to, ask the apparition to be specific with the message.

- There are several doorways in the spiritual realm. Be careful of the ones you open.

Read through all the rules again and again until they are resounding in your head. Do not try to contact the spiritual realm until you are confident you have mastered these rules. It is key to doing your mediumship the right way. A well-coordinated preparation isn't complete until you have double-checked the rule. Learning the rule is one thing, but compliance is another thing entirely. Follow everything discussed.

Technique 1: Formal Contact with Spirit

You have learned how to prepare for the spirit world spiritually. Physical preparation is also a must. There are specific considerations you must put in place for a comfortable environment. The venue must be cohesive and user-friendly. That does not mean you must be overly concerned with all the minor details. But naturally, there are things you should do.

- Consider contacting the spirit world in the evening – 8:00 is an excellent time for the session.

- Write down your questions for the spirit.

- Select the spirit to be contacted.

- Choose a quiet room with a table in the center.

- Disconnect all the radios, televisions, telephones, and stereos in your building.

- Tape a "Do Not Disturb" note to the door of your practice room.

- Dim the lights in the room. Turn them off if they can't be dimmed. Light two scented candles so you can have enough illumination in the room.

- You may add a bowl of flowers to the table if the spirit wants one.

- Place a bowl of water on the table - spirits sometimes communicate through the water.

- Add a bowl of hard candy to the table - they are great for accessing instant energy.

Now, you are at the point of summoning a spirit from the otherworldly realm. The most advanced mediums have used these steps for years. If you follow them as laid out, they will undoubtedly work for you. Never forget that intention is key to successful contact.

1. Sit in front of the table. Put yourself in a relaxed and calm state by focusing on stimulating thoughts.

2. Focus on breathing exercises for at least 10 minutes. Breathe as deeply as you can until you are confident you are in the right mental state to begin.

3. Place your palms down on the table. Spread your fingers out flatly to channel energy through your hands.

4. Now, recite your protection oath to form to reinforce the protective shell around you. Repeat the oat three times as you raise your vibration to induce a trance. Ensure your eyes are closed.

5. Once you are in a trance, call on your spirit guide to be part of the session. Some sensations you will get when your guide arrives include tingling, face stroking, ringing in your ears, and whispers around the room. You may even receive a vision at that moment.

6. Call out to the spirit you seek communication within a firm but calm tone. "Dearly departed, do you come with a message for me?" "Please come through to me." "I am ready for you." "May I ask questions?"

Sometimes, you may need to repeat your questions a couple of times. Don't start talking until you receive a mental image showing that the spirit is pleased to be in your presence. You may talk when the spirit initiates communication.

It is best not to be impatient. If the contact isn't immediate, don't force it. You cannot force the flow. Even as the spirit is in your presence, keep raising your vibrational level. Doing that will prevent an abrupt disconnection from the spirit world or the ghost with you.

When you feel like you have achieved your goal, you can conclude the session using the oath of conclusion.

"I thank you for the knowledge you have given. Thank you"

If the spirit refuses to leave:

"Thank you for joining me, but it is time to leave. Go with my love as your life is over. Leave me with my life. Go with love and light."

That's it - you have successfully contacted and communicated with an entity from the spirit world.

Remember two vital things: there are spirits and ghosts everywhere in the spiritual planes (parallel dimension), and the reality you create for spirits in this dimension is the only one they have. By raising the intensity of your vibrational level and your faith, you can attract any spirit you want to this dimension.

Why do you need the presence of your spirit guide before contacting the spirit world?

As a beginner, you may need extra help to strengthen your connection to the cosmic dimensions. Through your mind, ask your guide to assist in contacting the departed soul you want. When you do this, your guide will go to where that spirit is and ask them if they are interested in meeting you. If the spirit agrees, he comes through the opening you created. Otherwise, you may experience some back and forth until they agree.

Understand that departed souls owe you nothing; therefore, they can choose not to come when you summon them. The ghost you want may have no desire to establish contact with this plane. Suppose that happens. There, you have to respect their wishes. Do not persist if you don't want to be viewed as a problem.

Technique 2: Mirror Gazing

The mirror-gazing method is also called Psychomanteum. The modern techniques I explain here draw on the original method, which started in ancient Greece. Many people have successfully used mirror-gazing to have contact with spirits. The original method from Greece is complicated and is for advanced mediums. It is a more simplified version just as effective for spirit communication.

This technique was conceptualized by Dr. Raymond Moody, a psychologist and philosopher who created the term "near-death experience." To practice his mirror-gazing technique, all you need is a mirror, nothing else. In the past, the ancient Greeks needed animal sacrifice to summon their dead ones. Psychomanteum is similar to the practice of scrying. The only difference between both is that scrying is done with the use of a crystal ball.

Several steps are involved in performing a successful mirror-gazing session to invoke a spirit or contact the spirit world. They include:

- **Food:** Consume no caffeine or dairy a day before your session. Fruit and vegetables will help put you in a peaceful state of mind.

- **Location:** Choose a quiet location for the session. If you have already set up the sacred psychic space, then that is perfect. Use that location.

- **Clothing:** Remove all jewelry from your body. Put on loose, comfortable clothing.

- **Mirror:** Place a full-length mirror in front of a comfortable chair. Set it so you can look at it without straining your eyes. Make sure you cannot see your reflection.

- **Chair:** Sit in the chair while giving your head support.

- **Posture:** Release the tension from your body and relax your posture.

- **Awareness:** Increase your awareness to ease into the transition.

- **Music:** Calm and soothe your spirit by listening to beautiful music for about 15 minutes. Doing this further stimulates awareness.

- **Memories:** Select one or more personal items of the departed you wish to contact. Hold them in your hands and let memories flood into your mind. Pictures, videos, and anything else associated with the spirit can help.

- **Candle:** Light a candle behind you. Dim the light in the room to the ideal level. Twilight is the best time to practice, so adjust the light accordingly.

After executing all the steps above in order, your arms may start to feel heavy, with your fingers experiencing intense tingling sensations. You will feel yourself slipping into a trance-like, meditative state. The mirror might take on a cloudy appearance as if you were looking at a cloudy sky. Remain passive at that moment. Doing anything to the contrary can jar you from your hypnagogic state and interfere with the connection you are establishing.

The experience may not last for more than one minute since you are a beginner. Advanced practitioners often have far longer experiences. Some experiences you can have through a mirror-gazing session include seeing departed spirits and possibly future events. Proper preparation is vital for successful mirror-gazing – ensure you follow all the instructions given.

As always, record the events of your mirror-gazing sessions. Practice at least once a week to improve your skills and communicate with different entities from the spiritual dimensions.

Chapter Ten: Finding Your Spirit Guides

"The thought that the world will go on without you, that you will become nothing, is very hard to take in."

—Thomas Nagel

Everyone has a spiritual team, regardless of personality or background. Spirit guides exist to help and assist you along your way to fulfilling your destiny. No matter where you are in life currently, spirit guides must send helpful messages. They are filled with infinite wisdom that can never run dry. These souls have lived multiple lifetimes in the past; therefore, they understand just how it feels to experience life.

Spirit guides can help you with anything you want. If something is important to you, then it is essential to them. They are your guides because they are filled with positive energy while alive, and even now, they are higher-dimensional beings. Should you be wondering how you can find your unique guides so you can drink in the fountain of their wisdom and communicate with them at will, I have an explanation for you.

There are different types of spirit guides. Some had existed as your guides long before you were born into this plane. Others joined your team as the need for them manifested in your life at different points. You also can add more guides to your team if you so wish. After all, they are your spiritual squad.

I mentioned previously that every human typically has a spiritual team that holds up to six guides. Each guide performs different duties and obligations. Here are the types of guides that make up your spiritual team.

- **Archangels**

Archangels lead the plane where angels reside. They are mighty beings with a vast energy signature. You can instantly feel their impact wherever they appear or visit. If an archangel appears in your presence, you are bound to feel a literal energy shift in the environment. Archangels typically specialize in something. Your archangel might have a specialty in healing. Archangel Raphael is generally recognized as the angel of healing, with the power to attend to countless people at a time.

- **Guardian Angels**

Unlike archangels, guardian angels are assigned exclusively to you. Everyone has at least three, all of which have dedicated their lives towards helping just you. Anytime you need immediate assistance, your guardian angels are the right guides to call upon. Their love for you is unconditional and everlasting. They will stand with you from beginning to end. Even when you make huge mistakes, they won't chastise you. Instead, they will find ways to work with you on rectifying the mistakes. Your guardian angels are nondenominational, meaning they work with you regardless of your spiritual beliefs or faith.

• Spirit Animal

Your spirit animal might be a pet that passed away and has now joined your spiritual team. A spirit animal will always be a part of your squad, even if you have never had a pet. What matters is that the animal has the wisdom to teach and guide you. A peacock in your spiritual team might teach you the beauty of your abilities, while a wolf may show you how to survive the world with them. Spirit animals may appear to you in a dream, on a coffee mug, or in your garden. You may call on them whenever you want comfort and company.

• Ascended Masters

Having an ascended master on your team is a great feeling. With the amount of wisdom and experience they gained while on the physical plane, they have the necessary facilities to help you advance spiritual growth and development. They can also help you build spiritual influence. Ascended masters are considered leaders in the spiritual dimensions and teachers to those in the physical dimension. All the masters work together to create harmony throughout the universe. Religion and culture do not define them.

• Departed Loved Ones

Loved ones that have passed away to the other side sometimes choose to be a part of one's spirit guides. Since they are now higher-dimensional beings, they can help you from the highest planes practically. They may send job opportunities and healthy relationships your way. A great grandmother that has long since passed on may be part of your spiritual team, whether you knew her in this life or not. Even spirits you don't know can join your team due to a desire to help you achieve greatness.

• Helper Angels

These are like freelancers you have on your team. They are just there to help you in tricky or specific situations. For example, they can help you find a new space for your business or help you make new friends.

It is a fact that spirit guides exist to help you through your journey in life. But one question I often get from inquisitive clients is, "Can spirit guides be wrong?"

The above question is a crucial and loaded one. Many people often wonder if spirit guides are indecisive. Can they tell you to go that way after telling you to go this way?

Don't ever believe for a minute that your spirit guides are indecisive or that they are confusing. Second, psychic development requires that you let your spirit guide you at all times. However, this is not as easy as it sounds. Every new psychic finds it challenging to trust the guidance from their intuition.

When you are not used to getting support from family or friends, trusting your guides can be challenging. If you feel overwhelmed and confused initially, remind yourself that you have other incredible helpers besides your spiritual squad.

For one, you have your Higher Self - also called your authentic self, inner being, or soul. When you seek spiritual guidance from your spirit team, your Higher Self is ever-present to inform your decisions. Your Higher Self is the wisest and most confident version of yourself.

Second, understand that your spirit guides will always work for your highest good. That is why they are part of your team. Therefore, they will never steer you in the wrong direction. But that does not mean they are entirely in charge of your life. You are still the ultimate controller of your life. The spirit guides are there to act as your supporting cast.

So, the answer to that question is no. Your guides will never point you in the right direction. But you might decide not to follow the path advised by your guides sometimes. That is also okay. Before you make any decision, remember that your spirit guides always work for your highest good. They want the best for you, and it reflects in their guidance.

Connect with Your Spirit Guides

There are practical strategies to connect with your guides. These are simple things you can integrate into your daily life. Connecting with your spiritual team is like learning how to use a new recipe. At first, you know nothing about what you are doing. But if you have the proper instructions and stick to them, you will master them in time. Here are some of the best and easiest ways to connect with your spiritual team.

1. Be More Mindful and Present

Receiving guidance from your spiritual team is impossible without mindfulness. Being present in your daily life is crucial to recognize the signs and messages sent from the higher planes. Most of the time, you miss the signs because you are too immersed in other activities or too worried about other things. Actively make time in your schedule and dedicate it to mindfulness practice. After meditation, use at least 15 minutes of your time to simply take in your environment and ground yourself on the Earth.

2. Watch Out for Signs

Whether you are taking the bus to work or driving down, always remind yourself that your guides have messages for you. Don't take your mind off it when you are taking your bath in the morning. The more you prepare yourself to receive signs, the faster you can recognize them when they arrive. It gets interesting – as your spiritual team senses you are more aware and watchful for their messages, more messages are sent to help you. Always pay attention when you have a big decision to make – the guidance increases in situations like that.

3. Keep a Spirit Guide Journal

The purpose of a spirit guide journal is to increase interactions between you and your guides. Do not use the journal for recording your progress for this purpose; get another journal. In your spirit guide journal, you can write letters to your team and ask for concrete spiritual assistance. Using your free will to seek guidance is powerful. You may also record signs from them in this remarkable journey.

Make it a weekly activity to write the guides a letter. Appreciate and show gratitude for their presence in your life. Think about anything they have helped with recently and send your thanks. Then, ask for help on a specific situation in the next few sentences. Throughout the rest of the week, look out for synchronicities regarding the situation for which you requested guidance.

4. Name Your Guides

Naming your guides, particularly your guardian angels, enhances your ability to connect with them. It makes them feel more real than they already are, plus names push you to connect more regularly. Giving them names makes you closer than ever to your guides. After working closely with them over time, you may even begin to unravel their personalities. Use intuition to decide on names for your guides, or simply allow yourself to be creative.

5. Use Psychic and Divination Tools

Tools such as tarot cards, pendulums, crystals, or Ouija boards can heighten your connection with the guides. For years, humans have been communicating with the spirit world through psychic tools. While I make it a rule to recommend no-tools training to new mediums, you can start using tools depending on where you are in your training. In the first few months of dedicated practice, staying away from divination tools is the best decision you could make. However, you may use them once you get the hang of mediumship and psychic development.

Other ways you can connect with your spirit guides include:

- Inviting them into your home
- Meeting them in dreams and daydreams
- Opening yourself up to unexpected visits
- Spirit guide meditation
- Walking in nature with them
- Creating artistic pieces with them or exercising with them
- Doing occasional questions and answers reading with the squad

Never forget to set the intention whenever you connect with a spirit guide. Seek their help, the intention, seek guidance, and trust in the answer you receive.

Did you know that you can go on dates with your spirit guide? Yes, you can. It is just like when you go on dates with someone you have just met to know them better.

Going on dates with your spirit guides is your way of building a relationship and bond with them. The key to forming a real connection with your guides is to treat your relationship with them like you treat all your other ones. This way, you can have fun while developing your psychic abilities.

Fifteen to thirty minutes is a reasonable time to spend with your guides. Since Mondays to Fridays are usually filled with work and other stuff, selecting Saturday for your weekly date with your psychic guides works well.

The first time you attempt doing this, the guide (s) might not appear to you. Instead, you might get a sense of energy around you. Another time, you might get a silhouette. Little by little, the guides will sooner or later reveal themselves to you.

Going on dates involves asking questions so you can get to know the person. Just as you would ask questions to know more about the person you have just met, you can also ask your guides questions. During your time with them, you may ask questions such as:

- What is your name?
- Can you reveal yourself to me?
- Did we spend a previous lifetime together?
- Why did you choose to be my guide?
- What information would you like to give me at this moment?

The more you know about the guides, the more comfortable you will connect and bond with them. Knowing and understanding your guides is a continuing process. Record the thoughts and impressions you receive from the guides on your "dates." You will likely have multiple guides, so set apart different sections for recording your interactions with each guide.

Below is a step-by-step instruction of how you can invite your spirit guide into your home and learn more about them.

• Set the Ambience

As with any psychic or spiritual ceremony, cleaning up your environment is the first step to inviting a spirit guide into your home. Your sacred space should be clean and well-organized, with no hint of clutter anywhere. Light one or two candles in the room, dim the light, and create a warm-looking space for your visitor. The mood in the room should be calm and peaceful. Add items that hold significant energy into the mix - they will help maintain a high vibration around you. More importantly, they will amplify the intention you set.

• Set the Intention

At this point, you must have realized that all spiritual endeavors require you to set a clear intention. The intention should specify whom you seek to connect with and your questions for them. With a clear focus, you can call in the most suited entities to inform you or answer the questions. If you desire self-healing, gentle, loving energy may be the right spirit to call. If you need profound spiritual teachings, calling an Ascended Master such as Buddha makes more sense. With a pure and straightforward directive, you can attract the pure energy of the most suited Guide to help you.

- **Practice Patience**

There is no rush in this process. It is easy and straightforward, yet some people try to hurry it. Do not be like this. Guides do not rush or hurry – they take their time in appearing and sending messages. Any information your guide has for you will wash over you as gently as a breeze. Avoid setting expectations. Start with patience and trust, and you will communicate with the spiritual forces around you.

- **Relax and Breathe**

Breathing is fundamental in psychic ceremonies and activities. It is the perfect way to get yourself in a mental state that resonates with the higher dimensional being you wish to connect. It is also the surest way to ground yourself into the present, which matters when connecting with guides. With every deep breath, your awareness deepens and becomes more relaxed. There is no strain nor stress. If you feel tense in your body, do a quick stretch to relieve the symptoms. Lying down also works, but you might go off to sleep if you get too comfortable. Opening the pathways to spirits requires you to achieve stillness of breath. In the spot where there is no mental chatter is where you will meet your guides.

- **Bless Yourself**

Blessing yourself and your space is a way of protecting yourself. As with any spiritual work, you have to seek protection when you meet your spirit guides. Imagine yourself in a stream of white light. Let the light wash away anything short of the highest good. When done, relaxed, and in the mental state to receive a higher being, request your guide to come forth.

- **Chant a Sacred Sound**

Chant "Om" to create an alignment between your energy and that of the Divine. The most sacred sound is your voice. Chanting a mantra is your way of reechoing the sounds of the cosmos. It raises your vibrations and attunes your spiritual energy to align with the most powerful energies in the universe. You will discover that chanting opens the gateway to your guides more quickly.

- **Go Through the Doorway**

As your sacred space is activated with deep breathing and "om" chanting, observe a shift in your energy and environment. This is the activation of your "light body," which will attract the guides to you. Your light body is the part of you that is made purely of spirit – focus on it. Imagine yourself walking into the spiritual dimension through an opened gateway. That is your entry to the location where you can meet your guides.

- **Invite the Guides In**

You can finally call in any of your spirit guides, be it your guardian angel or helper angel. Share your intention and permit them to join you if they wish. If you do not give explicit permission, the spirit will stay away until you have. Give a command or an express invitation. Otherwise, you will spend your time in the sacred space alone.

- **Open to Subtle Frequencies**

Their interactions with you may come as impressions, visions, thoughts, or smells. The messages may not always be explicitly clear. Pay attention to every feeling and thought you get during your time with them. That is their way of directly communicating with you.

- **Ask Them to Show a Sign**

To be sure that you are indeed in the company of your spirit guide, ask them to show you signs. Asking is not equal to telling them what to do. Instead, your way of getting assurance that your faith and trust in them can become even stronger. They will happily oblige anything you ask.

- **Ask for a Blessing**

On your first meeting or date, it is permissible to ask for a blessing or message. Remember that your spirit guides serve you, and as such, they can only assist in the ways you ask them. While you are still connected, ask for guidance, insight, or a sneak peek at what the future holds for you. You may ask the guide to activate your mediumship skills to accelerate your psychic development process.

- **Show Gratitude**

Everyone loves to be appreciated. It feels great to hear "thanks" from someone you have just helped. So, give thanks to your guide for taking their time to meet you and impart divine guidance. Expressing gratitude might seem like a small act, but it is the best way to incur their goodwill and ensure they show up on your next date.

- **Return**

Through the same doorway you came through, return to this dimension. Going back to the way you came in is extremely important. Wait for some minutes until you are fully back into your material form. Record the experience in your journal, and then take a nap. Open yourself up to receive the experience at every level of your physical being.

The sacred space where you have the first meeting is the same place you will go back to anytime you seek communication with your spirit guide. Don't just go when you need help – sometimes, visit so that you can spend time with your spiritual team.

Conclusively, do not attempt to call all your guides at once. Your energy vibration cannot handle it. The highest number of spirits to invite at once should be two. You may increase this number as you advance in your spiritual learning journey. In time, your ability to receive intuitive and psychic messages will develop beyond the ritual, and soon, you will begin to get messages all the time – ritual or no ritual.

Chapter Eleven: Working in Spirit Circles

"Death is an entrance to experience rather than an exit from it."
—Charles Lindbergh

Psychic development is not an easy journey. It is not something many people understand. Unless you were raised in a home with an inclination toward spirits, you might not have family members and friends to act as your spiritual support system. Still, it is essential to have people who share similar interests with you. Together, you can work on becoming the best version of yourself. But how do you find people like that? That is the work of a spirit circle.

A spirit circle is a spiritual development group consisting of 6 to 8 people with a collective aim to develop themselves mentally, emotionally, and spiritually. As a new medium, joining a spirit circle is candidly the best step you can take toward achieving your journey alone. Without like-minded spirits to inform and guide your ways, you may not know when doing something the wrong way.

Joining a circle helps you come together in spirit and further a common interest. But you can do more than just that. In a development group, you can talk and relay experiences about your spiritual journey. Getting insight from people who have been in the same situation you are now is one benefit of joining a spiritual development circle.

In the group, members can also practice every technique, method, and secret they have learned about mediumship and psychic development. Someone may teach you a new method you don't know about yet, or you may even be the one to help your spiritual partners with the information they don't have yet.

A circle is meant to be a transformational plane where you can create time and space for healing. There is usually an advanced medium who is more experienced than everyone else in a circle. The medium can help beginners with healing and guidance to make their journey more tolerable and enjoyable.

Another benefit is that a development circle is a place for members to teach in turn. You don't have to know a lot but just know enough. Teaching your partners is the key to informing yourself and learning more. When you teach a particular method to your group, you increase your knowledge of that method or topic in general.

Do not juxtapose a spirit circle with a class – they are different. A class is a place for you to learn from another person about their spiritual way. There is usually no discussion. But a circle involves weekly or monthly sessions where one or more persons teach the rest of the group. But ultimately, the decision-making lies with all or most members.

Being a new medium, you might not find an existing circle to join. Since spiritual circles must not have over eight members, you are unlikely to find a group with an opening for you. This means you must form your own circle or partner with another person to form the group. Your skills level does not matter. What matters is the companionship you will be offering other new psychics and mediums like you.

However, as a beginner, you cannot manage a spirit circle on your own. Until you get to a certain point in your journey, you will need to find an advanced medium. This medium should be a veteran interested in helping other people develop their gifts and move forward in their journey.

Think about the structure of your spirit circle before you form one. Some of these decisions must be made before the circle's first physical meeting. Meanwhile, you can discuss with other members on the internet. There are networking apps for psychics to connect and discuss spiritual development together. The right thing to do is link up with psychics and mediums around your local area and see who is interested in joining your development group.

Do not set up your first meeting until you have discussed and agreed on the group's structure. Too often, I have seen people set up spirit circles with no sense of direction. If you follow this path, your group may end up splitting up.

As the pioneer, be the one to figure the structure out. You already know that you shouldn't have over eight members. Think about other things, such as the number of hours you would like to invest every week. Consult with everyone and choose a day that works for you and everybody else. A typical circle lasts up to two hours, during which you can practice a variety of psychic skills. The group can even do a séance together.

What are the things to clarify when deciding the circle structure?

- How often will the circle meet, where, and how long?
- Who will be the facilitator or facilitators of the circle?
- What are the activities to engage in on a rotational basis?
- Will there be a fee? What will the money be used for?
- Who is in charge of sending reminders to participants?

- Will there be a prerequisite for the group?
- What level of commitment does the circle expect from members?
- Can members come late or leave early?
- How deep will the practices go?

There should be a format that details which skills will be practiced first and when. To prevent things from getting boring, consider rotating the skills each week. The format in most circles is usually categorized into two areas: personal development and spiritual development.

The personal development segment is all about sharpening your thinking, reasoning ability, and developing a more significant emotional understanding capacity. The spiritual development sessions aim to understand the nature of the universe and commit to your relationship with your Higher Self and the Divine.

Create and print out a circle format that all participants can easily understand in the group. Remember that the participants can be of any background, but it is best to be 18 years of age. The format should suit the level of understanding of all members. Most important, every practice must be geared towards balancing personal and spiritual development. Highlight that spiritual development is a unique and personal process and that, therefore, participants should improve their skills rather than try to be better than other members.

A standard spirit circle format should include:

- **Opening Prayer:** Recite this at the beginning to express gratitude to the Divine for your life experiences and physical/spiritual wellbeing. The prayer should involve everyone.

- **Meditation:** Participants must learn to still their minds in anticipation of spiritual experiences, which makes meditation a vital part of the process. There are many benefits of having a relaxed body and a still mind, as you have already learned.

- **Spiritual Readings**: Participants should do readings on one another to develop their ability to communicate with spirit.

- **Healing:** Members should channel healing energy between one another. It can help strengthen their hands-on healing ability.

- **Pendulum Reading:** Pendulums can channel and invoke spirits. Together, members can learn how to use it to communicate with their guides and other spirits.

- **Aura Reading:** Together, members can practice reading energy by working on one another's energy fields. You can create an outline or guideline of the steps involved in aura reading.

Furthermore, you can practice developing your psychic senses of clairvoyance, clairsentience, clairaudience, claircognizance, clairgustance, and clairalience. Psychic skills such as telepathy, psychometry, mediumship, etc., should also be on the roster for members to develop.

There are crucial elements to make your spiritual circle function as you wish.

The first thing is to clarify the purpose and method of the circle. That might seem like an obvious thing, but it helps to highlight it. No one wants to spend valuable time driving across from town to discover that their mediumship circle represents Druidry. Don't make people feel like the circle is a waste of time.

Second, there must be integrity and transparency in the setup of the group's structure. The power structure should be clear to members to facilitate a clear flow of power. Clarifying the structure to all is key to developing the circle members' bond. It also helps to prevent miscommunication and unnecessary conflicts. Conflicts are not avoidable, so you must have resolution guidelines set in place.

Members can leave at any time, so the group should be open to other people to come in. The structure should remain the same regardless of who goes and who joins. A formal power structure in place to encourage power-sharing will prevent misuse of power by power-holding members.

You will realize that each circle has its spirit. The more you meet, the stronger the spirit will become. Advise members to tap into the guiding force of the collective spirit to strengthen their energy.

A spirit circle's objective is to allow participants to develop their psychic, spiritual, and mediumship gifts continuously. Each week, work on different things with members. Members should also share their individual experiences in their journey to inspire and motivate other members to keep going.

You can learn to connect with your spirit guides and loved ones who have passed on to the other dimension with like-minded individuals.

An excellent app for meeting people who might want to join your spirit circle is the Amino for Witches and Pagans app, which is available to install on Google Playstore and Apple store. There are beginner groups on the app where you can connect with those who have just begun their mediumship journey like you. There are also advanced-members groups where you can meet established mediums and psychics. There, you may be able to find an advanced medium willing to be part of your spirit circle.

Chapter Twelve: Enhance Your Psychic Powers

"One of the most useful and important ways to be able to use your psychic gifts is to learn how to read what is happening in your own very body."

—Catherine Carrigan

You can enhance your psychic powers in a variety of ways. This chapter focuses on two things you can do to further your psychic powers - claircognizance and using essential oils.

Claircognizance is the gift of inner knowing. It enables you to intuitively know things in ways devoid of reason and logic. A claircognizant experience will leave you wondering, "Woah, how did I know that?"

Psychical knowing is a superb ability that can make a difference in your psychic journey. You have possibly had claircognizant experiences. Think about that time you decided not to take your usual route to work, only to discover there was a long traffic jam along that way. Or maybe you knew not to feed your new puppy a specific meal brand, only to discover they are allergic to one ingredient.

Claircognizance has likely manifested itself in your life through different channels. Let's dive into how it can help you further your psychic development and mediumship journey.

Often, people confuse claircognizance and clairsentience for each other. This happens because both psychic skills get presented as "gut feelings." Distinguishing between the two is essential. If you don't, it may confuse which one is your dominant psychic ability.

The psychic gift of inner feeling allows you to feel that someone might be dishonest, while inner knowing lets you know. Feeling differs from knowing. When convinced about someone or something, you can't shake your conviction; this is considered claircognizance. But clairsentience is when you feel strongly about something. The feelings may be fleeting, but they come to you.

Those who are claircognizant receive intuitive messages in three ways. The first way is via their gut feelings. The inner knowing sometimes comes from your guts. Unless you have experienced something like that before, describing it can be difficult. Those with the gift find it hard to describe or explain that they have no logical explanation. They opt to describe it as a "gut feeling" because that is a concept that most people can grasp, psychic or not. However, claircognizant messages may feel like they come from your guts because this psychic sense is linked to your solar plexus, which is around your guts.

Claircognizant messages sometimes come "out of the blue," meaning you don't know the source or origin. They just "pop" into people's heads from nowhere, leaving them surprised. They often come while you are engaged in an activity entirely unrelated and disrupts your thinking. You might be in the bathroom getting ready for work, and then the thought pops into your head, "Let me take another route to work today." Then when you discover that your usual route was blocked, you wonder why that thought popped into your head earlier.

The third way that claircognizant messages are received is in the sleep state. For example, you go to bed thinking about a business problem you have to solve. Suddenly, you awaken from your sleep with a brilliant solution in mind. "I wasn't even thinking. Where did this come from?" This particular experience has happened to me many times. You just wake up knowing things with no idea how they got to your mind or when.

Realistically, the idea of receiving messages that can't logically be explained to anyone is a little bit frightening. And it might even affect your social life. Imagine yelling "STOP" to your friend who is about to have a lousy drink unknowingly. Of course, they will regard you strangely even if they will thank you later.

Like all intuitive messages, claircognizant messages come from the spirit guides, your spiritual team, and your Higher Self. Once you are far developed in your psychic practice, you will understand the exact being responsible for the messages you receive. You may find yourself receiving messages you don't know how to deal with. There, the meanings will come to you over time.

Here are signs you may be claircognizant:

- You know when someone is insincere or fake
- You often awake with brilliant solutions to challenging problems
- You receive intuitive hits out of the blue, and they always end up being right

Even if claircognizance is not your primary psychic gift, you still have it in you. So, you can work on developing it regardless.

Claircognizance training can be done in many ways, but you can focus on two of the most effective methods. The first is to seek your spirit guides' help, while the second involves using visualization exercises to hone your skills. As a bonus, there is another method which you will find below.

Developing Claircognizance helped by your Spirit Guides

You have already learned how to contact your spirit guides, but how can you invite them to develop a specific psychic ability?

• Invite your spirit guide using the instructions in Chapter Ten.

• Set the intention you seek the help of your guide in developing your claircognizance gift.

• Call forth to your spirit guide.

• Ask them to give you guidance in honing your intuitive gifts.

• Thank them for honoring your invitation and obliging your request.

Use crystals and essential oils during the sessions with your spirit guides.

Claircognizance Visualization Exercise

This exercise should be combined with journaling to get the best results.

• Take out your journal and pen.

• Write about how you see yourself when you have fine-tuned and increased your claircognizance gift.

• Describe an aspect of your life where you would like to make a change and a positive impact.

• Visualize how your inner knowing gift will make you feel and how it can affect your daily life.

• Meditate on the day you just described for yourself. Then, picture it in wholesome details.

• Immerse yourself in the moment and visualize how you feel when you have a claircognizant experience.

Be specific with the meditation to increase your claircognizance.

Automatic Writing

Automatic writing or, if you prefer, freewriting is a productive and fun way of training your claircognizant sense. With this exercise, you can attune to your inner knowing gift. At the start of your psychic development journey, you will second-guess your gut feelings. Freewriting allows you to gain confidence in the messages you receive, and more importantly, get direct answers from your spirit guides and your Higher Self.

Here is how you can train with automatic writing:

- Grab your notebook and a pen. Before you write, ask your spirit guides a question.

- Place your pen on the paper and write down anything that comes to you. Just write and go with the flow, even if you think it is gibberish.

The writing may not make much sense to you immediately, so give it time. Over the next few days or weeks, the meaning will come to you gradually. On your first few tries, this automatic writing exercise might seem absurd to you. However, those first tries are to clear out your subconscious until it is ready to receive valuable information. Soon, your notes will be filled with things that make absolute sense to you. You will receive clear and concise claircognizant messages, and your psychic knowing skill will advance.

Essential Oils

Essential oils have several kinds of excellent benefits for upcoming and established psychic mediums. The right oil combinations can help you achieve many of your intuitive abilities. They are a must for anyone looking to train themselves in mediumships. Whether you apply them to your skin or rub on your crystals, there is more than one way to reap their benefits.

Here's the thing – you can't just apply essential oils and expect them to start enhancing your psychic powers. You have to set the intention. Intention setting is key to psychic rituals and ceremonies.

All essential oils have multiple functions, and they all work for psychic development. But the fact remains that some of these oils are more effective than others. Again, your intention must be clarified for you to reap the power-boosting benefits.

There are tons of oils, but how do you know which ones will be good for you? Before I go ahead, please understand that there are no perfect oils. Don't overwhelm yourself trying to choose perfect ones. Instead, let your intuition guide you toward the oils that will benefit you the most. Also, try the oils you feel connected to than others.

The following are the best oils for grounding and centering yourself while enhancing your intuition and sense of clarity. You have the liberty of changing the oils to use based on your mood, activity, and season.

1. Cedarwood: Mental decluttering is super vital in psychic training. This essential oil can help you get rid of mental clutter to gain the ultimate clarity your soul needs. Add it to your collection.

2. Rose Essential Oil: To strengthen your connection with your Higher Self while increasing harmony between all your six psychic senses, this is the oil for you. Rose oil can amplify your abilities to a considerable extent, and the effects are not temporary.

3. Lemon Oil: I am convinced that every psychic has lemon oil in their collection. Its benefits are simply too incredible for you to leave it out of your list. The vibrant citrus smell helps to promote an alert and present mind, which you need during psychic exercises training.

4. Chamomile: Drinking chamomile tea is good, but the oil is even better. Like the tea, chamomile has a powerful calming effect that can help release your mind from fears and open it to the truth. If you are doubtful or scared of your abilities, diffuse some chamomile into your bath water or rub it on your skin. The fear will be eradicated.

5. Peppermint Oil: Most psychic mediums add peppermint oil to their collection because of its great smell, but that is not the only reason. That smell is responsible for its immediate awakening of the mind to increase focus. It is so powerful that having it around can help you concentrate when communicating with spirits. The scent peppermint gives your home will just be an added benefit.

6. Lavender Oil: This oil is often recommended as a remedy for sleep due to its calmness-inducing properties. It can help you relax and let go of control when contacting your spirit guides. It is the right oil to diffuse during journaling or visualization practice.

7. Frankincense: The fantastic grounding properties in this oil is one reason it should be a part of your daily routine. Use it whenever you feel out of touch from your inner psychic.

8. Rosemary: This essential oil is a perfect alternative for sage. If you don't like the smell of burning sage, go for rosemary oil to keep harmful spirits and energies out of your life. Plus, you can use it to open your third eye and enhance clairvoyance.

9. Jasmine: Remember that psychic messages sometimes come in the dream state? Well, this is the perfect oil to help you receive more precise messages in your dreams and daydreams. Diffuse some jasmine oil before you go to bed every night to remember dream visits more clearly.

10. Sandalwood: This is one oil that has potent purifying properties. You can use sandalwood to release yourself from your past negativity – a crucial step to psychic awakening.

The best thing about essential oils is that you can apply them anytime you choose. Below is a simple exercise to use your essential oils safely and correctly.

- Sit in your sacred meditative spot.
- Get six drops of your chosen oil in your diffuser and concentrate internally.
- Do a simple meditation and set your intention.
- Try one of the psychic exercises you have learned in this book.
- Do some journaling or more meditation to commune with your spirit guides.

Some other ways you can use the essential oils include:

- Diffusing before you begin any activity.
- Dropping a little oil into your bathwater.
- Sprinkling on a fabric, then put under your pillow before you sleep.
- Add a little essential oil to a carrier oil and rub in the spots where you usually apply your perfume.

The psychic journey to mediumship is not something that you can master in one weekend. Give room for growth as you practice. Allow yourself to experiment, fail, and try again. Remember that psychic development can sometimes take years.

Conclusion

Mediumship is an interesting and awesome gift to master. The first few times you connect with the spirit world may leave you in awe. You may feel like you have no control over what you receive. Or maybe you don't feel a flow in your readings. No matter how you feel at the beginning, you will come to enjoy and appreciate your gift. That you can affect your life and the whole universe with your gift will keep you inspired as you go through the process of training.

Here's another book by Mari Silva
that you might like

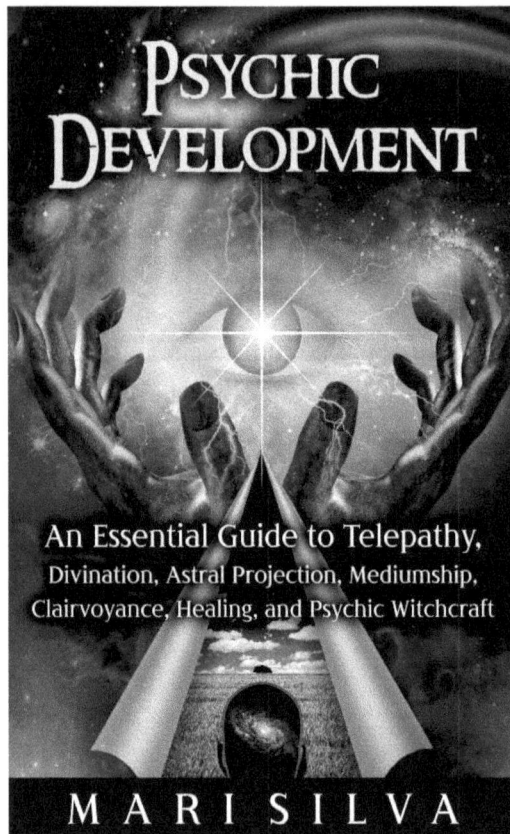

PSYCHIC
DEVELOPMENT

An Essential Guide to Telepathy,
Divination, Astral Projection, Mediumship,
Clairvoyance, Healing, and Psychic Witchcraft

MARI SILVA

Your Free Gift (only available for a limited time)

Thanks for getting this book! If you want to learn more about various spirituality topics, then join Mari Silva's community and get a free guided meditation MP3 for awakening your third eye. This guided meditation mp3 is designed to open and strengthen ones third eye so you can experience a higher state of consciousness. Simply visit the link below the image to get started.

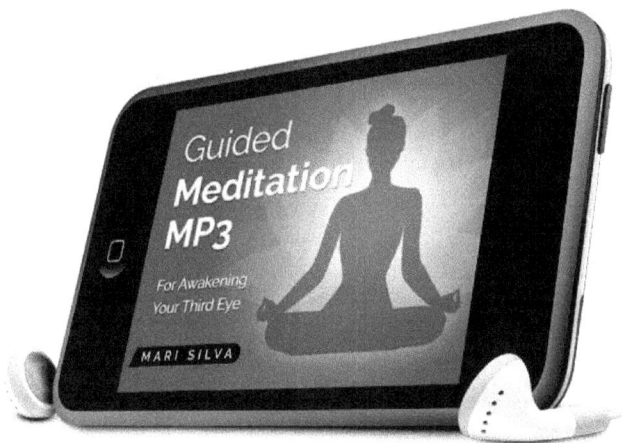

https://spiritualityspot.com/meditation

References

Clairvoyance | psychology. (n.d.). Encyclopedia Britannica.
https://www.britannica.com/topic/clairvoyance

Doors To Other Worlds by Buckland, Raymond. (n.d.). Www.biblio.com.
https://www.biblio.com/doors-to-other-worlds-by-buckland-raymond/work/991425

Medium | occultism. (n.d.). Encyclopedia Britannica.
https://www.britannica.com/topic/medium-occultism

Mediumship Quotes (14 quotes). (n.d.). Www.goodreads.com.
https://www.goodreads.com/quotes/tag/mediumship

ThriftBooks. (n.d.). Reunions: Visionary Encounters with... book by Raymond A.
Moody Jr. ThriftBooks. https://www.thriftbooks.com/w/reunions-visionary-
encounters-with-departed-loved-ones_raymond-a-moody-
jr/292870/#edition=2269514&idiq=1005995